SNATCHED FROM THE JAWS OF THE LION

The story of a woman's journey from Spiritism to Christianity,

AND HER EXAMINATION OF THE SPIRITIST PRACTICES USED IN THE POPULAR DEVOTIONALS, THE COURSE IN MIRACLES, GOD CALLING, AND JESUS CALLING

. . . the Master stood by me and helped me spread the Message loud and clear to those who had never heard it. I was snatched from the jaws of the lion! God's looking after me, keeping me safe in the kingdom of heaven. All praise to Him, praise forever! Oh, yes!
2 TIMOTHY 4: 17-18 (TM)

Come and hear, all who fear God,
And I will tell of what He has done for my soul.
PSALM 66: 16

ELIZABETH BRYANT

ISBN: 1490300260
ISBN 13: 9781490300269

This work is lovingly dedicated to the memory of the one who gave me birth, and to the Savior who gave us both second births. May we spend eternity singing His praises together!!

Scripture quotations are taken from the New American Standard Bible, 1995 Update (NASB95), unless otherwise noted.
New American Standard Bible: 1995 Update. LaHabra, CA: The Lockman Foundation, 1995.

The following versions are also used and noted in portions of the text.
Peterson, Eugene H. *The Message: The Bible in Contemporary Language.* Colorado Springs, CO: NavPress, 2005.

The New King James Version. Nashville: Thomas Nelson, 1982.

The Holy Bible: New Revised Standard Version. Nashville: Thomas Nelson Publishers, 1989.

The Holy Bible: English Standard Version. Wheaton: Standard Bible Society, 2001.

The Holy Bible: New International Version. Grand Rapids, MI: Zondervan, 1984.

All forms of emphasis in the quotes or Scriptures are mine unless otherwise noted.

ACKNOWLEDGEMENTS

The culmination of this work has come with tears and gratitude. God has been faithful to me and has brought me thus far. When I began writing, I had no idea how God could use this work, or even if I would ever complete it. All along the way, the Lord has caressed me with His Scripture and fueled me with a greater love for His people than for my own privacy. He has led through people I love dearly to ask the questions, spot the errors, and encourage me along the way. They have been used of the Lord to lavish His grace upon me and to generously meet the needs of my heart.

Friends who prayed, and prayed, and prayed for me and my family as I worked on the book have had a great part in the birthing process. Thanks to the Brokenness Prayer Group for their prayerful support and to all the others who cried with me and supported me throughout the endeavor.

My two daughters and their husbands, Beka and Matt and Kay and Tim, aided greatly by putting up with endless discussions about the book's progress, reading update after update of the "latest" edition, and praying for me as I wrote. I so valued their wise input and trusted their responses to the text.

My daughter, Kay, and Ann, my sister-in-law, were my A-team editors who encouraged me, helped organize the text, and asked the difficult questions that made me look deeper into the subject matter. These dear people gave of their time, gifting, and energies to make this book a reality. They shared my vision and helped to carry me to the goal.

I am greatly indebted to Tom, my wonderful husband of 44 years, for his faithful support and focused editing of draft after draft of this book. How can I thank him enough! Tom believed that this was a worthy work and encouraged me to keep on keeping on, in spite of set-backs and discouragements. He edited, and edited, and edited again, long past what is considered normal endurance. He prayed with me and for me, and patiently endured my interruptions and passionately embraced my mission. I am so blessed to have a husband who has shown me through the years that his family is his top priority.

And most importantly, I owe all to my precious Lord and Savior, who answered every prayer and took care of every concern. My gratitude will ever flow to Him for all He has done on my behalf and on behalf of those I love. He did abundantly beyond all that I asked or even thought to ask. To Him be all the glory and honor.

Elizabeth Bryant

TABLE OF CONTENTS

PSALM 71 9

PREFACE 11

I SATAN'S HOLD 13

II I AM SAVED! 19

III SNARED BY THE DECEIVER 33

IV MY DETOUR 41

V A MIRACLE OF FORGIVENESS 55

VI THE CALL: THE MIRACLE BEGINS! 63

VII WEEK ONE: STRUGGLE 79

VIII THE MIRACLE WEEK 89

IX HOME 103

X JOURNEY TO THE END 119

XI THE FINAL WEEK 123

XII THE GRAND ADVENTURE 131

APPENDIX 137

PSALM 71

I run for dear life to God, I'll never live to regret it. Do what you do so well: get me out of this mess and up on my feet. Put your ear to the ground and listen, give me space for salvation. Be a guest room where I can retreat; you said your door was always open! You're my salvation—my vast, granite fortress. My God, free me from the grip of Wicked, from the clutch of Bad and Bully. You keep me going when times are tough— my bedrock, God, since my childhood. I've hung on you from the day of my birth, the day you took me from the cradle; I'll never run out of praise.

Many gasp in alarm when they see me, but you take me in stride. Just as each day brims with your beauty, my mouth brims with praise. But don't turn me out to pasture when I'm old or put me on the shelf when I can't pull my weight. My enemies are talking behind my back, watching for their chance to knife me. The gossip is: "God has abandoned him. Pounce on him now; no one will help him."

God, don't just watch from the sidelines. Come on! Run to my side! My accusers—make them lose face. Those out to get me—make them look like idiots, while I stretch out, reaching for you, and daily add praise to praise. I'll write the book on your righteousness, talk up your salvation the livelong day, never run out of good things to write or say. I come in the power of the Lord God, I post signs marking his right-of-way.

You got me when I was an unformed youth, God, and taught me everything I know. Now I'm telling the world your wonders; I'll keep at it until I'm old and gray. God, don't walk off and leave me until I get out the news of your strong right arm to this world, news of your power to the world yet to come, your famous and righteous ways, O God. God, you've done it all! Who is quite like you? You, who made me stare trouble in the face, Turn me around; Now let me look life in the face. I've been to the bottom; Bring me up, streaming with honors; turn to me, be tender to me,

And I'll take up the lute and thank you to the tune of your faithfulness, God. I'll make music for you on a harp, Holy One of Israel. When I open up in song to you, I let out lungs-full of praise, my rescued life a song. All day long I'm (talking) about you and your righteous ways, While those who tried to do me in slink off looking ashamed.

The Message

PREFACE

Put your ear to the ground and listen, give me space for salvation.
Psalm 71:2 (TM)

One day in 2011, I left my favorite Christian bookstore, disturbed and upset. One of the most popular devotional books of our time, Sarah Young's *Jesus Calling*[1], was prominently displayed on the store's shelves. What is so disturbing about that? In order to understand my concern, you must know a portion of my life story, which I began writing a year before this event. Follow me through the years and see why a book so highly regarded by many in the Christian community caused me so much concern. I began recording my story on a winter morning in 2010 . . .

The snow is swirling in the worst blizzard Northern Virginia has seen in fourteen years. There are thirty inches of the cold, wet stuff on the ground with another twenty inches predicted. This is what welcomed me when I returned home from Jackson, Mississippi, where I witnessed one of the greatest miracles of my life!

I must record the wonder of a God who never forgets a prayer nor neglects a tear shed for the lost. The undulating snow outside reminds me that God can take the twisted circumstances of life and weave a pattern from the hopelessness of man, breathing His Holy Spirit on brokenness, and leaving something beautifully breathtaking in its place.

As I sit at my desk with a full mug of hot coffee and my computer on "ready," I am enveloped in a sense of reverent warmth as my memories mimic the complexity of the whirling snow outside my window. I wonder if I can even describe these events without soiling the beauty and majesty of God's magnificent work with my clumsy and awkward words.

Wednesday, February 10, 2010

---

[1] Young, Sarah. *Jesus Calling, Enjoying Peace in His Presence.* Nashville, TN: Thomas Nelson, 2004.

I
SATAN'S HOLD

My God, free me from the grip of Wicked, from the clutch of Bad and Bully.
Psalm 71:4 (TM)

This is the story of two women who were both *snatched from the jaws of the lion.* One was liberated at the age of 23; the other experienced her freedom just a year before her death at the age of 80. It is a true story of a mother and daughter who wanted the same thing, a relationship with God. However, they sought that goal in two distinctly different ways but, ultimately, joined their hearts for a brief time in a kinship beyond the familial. Both questioned the validity of their learned practices and influences, while choosing opposing directions in their lives. By doing so, their spiritual understanding was divided on the most important question known to man: *Who do you say Jesus is?* Not only was the theological gap widened between the two women, but also there were clefts in their mother-daughter relationship as well. The Truth and a lie were both contending for their hearts. In the end, the Truth emerged victoriously, for the Truth is what set them both free.

Although I consider this a victorious journey that began in 1974, as I look back, I must acknowledge several events that affected my life and brought me to what I consider a significant miracle. My story begins many years before my birth, and involves previous generations in my family. To appreciate what happened, the reader needs to be aware of the satanic crafts that permeated my heritage and the early years of my life. As a result of our family situation, I grew up in the same house with my maternal grandmother, yet I was unaware of the strong impact her beliefs would have on my mother, my siblings, and me.

While she did not fit the stereotypical, Hollywood character of a turbaned charlatan or a gypsy fortuneteller, nevertheless, my grandmother was a medium! My memories are of a gray-haired grandmother who loved my brother and me and thought of us as her own. Unfortunately, she also acted as a channel of communication between living human beings on earth and, what she believed to be, dead persons in the spirit world. Thomas Overholt, in his *Cultural Anthropology and the Old Testament,* translates the Hebrew word "medium" from 1 Samuel 28:7 as "mistress of a ghost."[2] Brooks Alexander, in his article, *What is Spiritism?,* explains:

> Mediums put themselves into a state of trance, more or less at will. In the trance state, spirits are contacted mentally and then invited to use the medium's body to speak through or otherwise relate to human beings. As one medium put it, "Mediumship is a form of voluntary possession." The function of the trance state is to disengage the medium's mind from involvement with the space time world by shutting out sensory input. This state permits contact with the nonphysical realm of spirits and also vacates control of the medium's physical faculties for use by the spirits themselves.[3]

This definition accurately describes my grandmother's practices as a medium or spiritist. She was a trance medium or channeler who 'contacted' whom she believed were dead persons by becoming passive, going into a trance, and then allowing an entity or familiar spirit to enter her body to speak through her. Grandmother was a 'closet' medium, as it was illegal to be a practicing medium in Missouri where my grandmother and her family lived. Therefore, Grandmother kept these so-called talents and skills secret to most people, except for a very limited few. She was, however, an active member of the Church of Unity, located in Lees Summit, Missouri. My mother followed in her mother's footsteps and also became a practicing medium or spiritist.

---

[2] Overholt, Thomas W. *Cultural Anthropology and the Old Testament.* Minneapolis: Fortress Press, 1996, 73.

[3] Alexander, Brooks. "What is Spiritism?". SCP Journal Vol. 7.1 (1987): 6.

John Ankerberg and John Weldon wrote about the Church of Unity in their *Encyclopedia of Cults and New Religions:*

> The Unity School is a pseudo-Christian sect founded by Myrtle and Charles Fillmore in 1889. It is based on a mixture of Christian terminology and pantheistic philosophies, particularly the late 1800s 'metaphysical' movement known as New Thought. Updated to reflect current New Age philosophies, the usual New Age menu of beliefs are included in Unity ideas – reincarnation, the divinity of self, a.k.a. Christ Consciousness, evil as illusory, love as all that is real, and so on. Spiritual practices from other religions, particularly Eastern religions, are affirmed, supported, and taught in Unity. Meanwhile, their particular interpretation of Christianity is emphasized.[4]

Walter Martin, in his classic book on the cults, *The Kingdom of the Cults,* states that Unity is "non-Christian on the basis that it violates every cardinal doctrine of the Christian faith necessary to salvation, as outlined within the pages of Scripture."[5]

At this point, I feel I must differentiate between two words that are frequently confused in discussions on this topic: *spiritism* and *spiritualism.* "*Spiritism* is a general term covering all types of spirit contact. *Spiritualism* is a more specific term which refers to a modern religious movement centered on contact with spirits of the dead through trance mediums."[6] This movement arose in the late 19th century and is prevalent today in a more organized form. The word Spiritualism is the terminology my family used as I was growing up, even though they were in reality, spiritists. The focus of the spiritists and Spiritualism is, again, contacting the dead through trance mediums or channelers.

Interestingly, a rise in spiritism has always followed a period of social crisis, such as a war. In an attempt to find comfort and

---

4 Ankerberg, John and John Weldon, *Encyclopedia of Cults and New Religions.* Eugene, OR: Harvest House, 1999, 540ff.

5 Martin, Walter, *The Kingdom of the Cults.* Minneapolis, MN: Bethany House Publishers, 1985, 279.

6 Alexander 7.

to continue a relationship with the dead, mediums have been sought out to provide a connection with deceased loved ones. The chaos resulting from the two World Wars during the 20th century did much to promote an increase in the number of mediums.

What began with a crystal ball in back, dimly lit rooms in whispered séances has moved into the cultural mainstream. The counterculture of the 1960s opened the door to even greater fascination with Eastern mystical spiritism, which was adopted by the New Age culture as we know it today. Proponents of the New Age movement include an array of Hollywood stars and others made notable by their exposure on popular TV talk shows. Although the beginnings of spiritism were on the social fringe, the cult has now moved to center stage. However, the Bible remains consistent in its rejection of any practice of spiritism, which would encompass modern day spiritualism and its now widely accepted New Age philosophies.

Spiritists are clearly condemned in the Scriptures (Lev. 19:31; 20:6; Deut. 18:11). Deuteronomy 18:10–12 emphatically states:

> "There shall not be found among you anyone who makes his son or his daughter pass through the fire, **one who uses divination, one who practices witchcraft, or one who interprets omens, or a sorcerer, or one who casts a spell, or a medium, or a spiritist, or one who calls up the dead. "For whoever does these things is detestable to the Lord;** and because of these detestable things the Lord your God will drive them out before you."

There is also a sham element associated with spiritists and mediums; however, Walter Martin asserts:

> Not all psychic or spiritistic phenomena can be exposed as fraudulent. There is a spiritual dimension which cannot be ignored. Authentic Spiritists draw their power from the one the Bible calls 'a roaring lion' who seeks 'whom he may devour' (1 Peter 5:8), who is Satan. Spiritism . . . directly contradicts the Bible, God's Word. As well as constituting something

> akin to consumer fraud, spiritism also constitutes Biblical heresy.[7]

Drs. Ankerberg and Weldon address the origin and the dangers of channeling:

> The first historical incidence of channeling is recorded in the Bible in Genesis Chapter 3. There in the Garden of Eden the devil used the serpent as a "channel" to trick Eve (Gen. 3:1-5; 2 Cor. 11:3; Rev. 12:9). Through channeling, the devil deceived man into doubting God, with serious consequences. Significantly, there are compelling reasons for believing that the basic reality of channeling that is suggested here has never altered, either as to its (1) origin (the devil or demons); (2) result (spiritual deception which undermines trust in God); (3) consequences (divine judgment; Gen. 3:13-19, Deut. 18:9-13). Channeling is thus condemned in the Bible as an evil practice before God. It is rejected because it is a form of spiritism which involves contact with demons and the spreading of their false teachings.
>
> The Bible further teaches that "in later times some will fall away from the faith, paying attention to deceitful spirits and doctrines of demons" (1 Tim. 4:1). Spiritistic teachings pervert the nature of God, lie about Christ and distort the way of salvation. Those who trust spiritistic teachings face judgment at death. On the authority of one no less that Christ Himself we discover that Hell is a real place (Matt. 25:46; Luke 16:19-31). The demons who assure men that sin is not real and Hell does not exist are bringing eternal ruin to those who trust them.
>
> The Bible instructs man to reject every form of spiritism as something evil and an encounter with lying spirits. Channeling is a form of spiritual warfare with the souls of men at stake (2 Cor. 4:4). This is why both

[7] Martin 228.

> channeling itself and following the teaching of the channelers are condemned in Scripture as rebellion against God and as courting His judgment. [8]

Brooks Alexander adds:

> The dominant theme of the Old Testament's ban on spiritism is defilement. The spirits are evil spirits – though, needless to say, they do not appear with fangs bared, barbed tails twitching, and hidden agendas displayed. All of this logically suggests that the spirits of spiritism are demonic. The Bible indeed affirms that they are, and the spirits themselves continually confirm it by the content of their messages.[9]

Although we did not speak of it openly in our family, the validity of reincarnation (the Hindu belief that one moves from one body to the next at death in an evolutionary process until reaching perfection) and many beliefs from other religions were all equally accepted. Talking to the dead (in reality, demonic spirits posing as the loved one) and seeing into the spirit world were all acceptable practices. This unholy mix of New Age and Christian philosophies was never challenged in my thinking at that time. I too was programmed with this New Age philosophy and even in the early years of my newfound faith in Christ, I attempted to reconcile the two opposing beliefs. As I grew as a Christian, I found that they could not be reconciled, but the former had to be renounced. My struggle to arrive at a clear understanding in this vital area is detailed in the following chapters.

---

[8] Ankerberg, John and John Weldon. *The Facts on Spirit Guides.* Harvest House Publishers, Eugene, OR. 1988. Pg. 25.

[9] Alexander 7.

II
I AM SAVED!

I run for dear life to God. I'll never live to regret it.
Do what you do so well: get me out of this mess and up on my feet.
Psalm 71:1 (TM)

It was 1974 and a hot and muggy summer Sunday in Hattiesburg, Mississippi. I was 23 years old and nervously waiting my turn to be baptized into the fellowship of Christians at the University Baptist Church. I felt strange in this unfamiliar setting, a traditional church, but this was the time and place when I first understood the true message of Christ's sacrifice rendered on my behalf. Only my God, my husband, and I knew how far I had come to be there in His presence and to accept His salvation plan. My being there was the beginning of the great miracle God would work in my own life. Let me set the stage for you.

I was the second child born in Kansas City, Missouri, to two 22-year-old 'children' who married at 18. Soon after my birth, their turbulent marriage resulted in an acrimonious divorce, and my father went West and my mother, brother, and I accompanied my grandparents South to northern Mississippi.

Hoping to fulfill my grandmother's passion for cooking and hospitality, and to be near her sisters, who lived close by in other Mississippi towns, my grandparents leased a restaurant in Eupora, Mississippi, at the intersection of State Highways 182 and 9. In 1954, after only three months of living in Eupora, my grandfather died. Grandmother then became the sole proprietor of the Eupora Café, as well as the matriarch of our small family.

During that time, my mother put her own personal dreams and desires on hold by helping my grandmother in the daily operation of the Eupora Café. Some of my earliest memories are the smell of food cooking, the sound of dishes rattling, jovial conversation among the staff, and the continual music of the jukebox in the background. I can still recall the odor of those vinyl restaurant booths as I would exhaustedly curl up in one to sleep on those nights my mother worked late. The kindness and warm smiles of the kitchen staff during our long hours there helped me to love all people, even in that highly segregated Mississippi environment.

Years later, I learned that Elvis Presley and his small entourage stopped by the Eupora Café one afternoon in the mid-1950s. He enjoyed my grandmother's cooking and even chatted and flirted with my young, pretty mother. Mother didn't even recognize him. Perhaps he was frustrated that she didn't know who he was, but as he was leaving, Elvis punched every button on the jukebox that was labeled with one of his popular songs. As they left the small town, the local sheriff, having seen the Presley entourage drive away, ran into the café all excited about the Tupelo native being in Eupora! Mother never told any of us children about the encounter until about a year before her death. She said that she was afraid people would think she was bragging. Mother was shy at the time of this encounter, and had not yet attained the self-confidence she would exhibit later in life.

While in Eupora, we lived across the street from a church. I must have attended Vacation Bible School there because in the family archives there are my plaster hand moulds that my grandmother saved from the event. I have no memory of making these, but I do remember that years later I had a surprising recall of Psalm 100. These memories came flooding back to me during the early years of marriage when my husband would recite various Psalms to me in order to soothe my troubled heart. There is no place I could have memorized God's Word other than VBS in Eupora. Even then, God's loving hand was directing my circumstances.

Later, we moved from Eupora to an even smaller Mississippi town, Okolona, where my grandmother made one last attempt at the restaurant business before finally giving up her dream altogether. As the restaurant experiment reluctantly ended for my grandmother, Mother had the opportunity to go to Memphis, Tennessee, where she looked for a job more suitable to her talents. My brother and I stayed in Okolona with Grandmother for an entire school year before Mother was able to have us live with her in Memphis.

Mother got a job with a printing company as a print setter and commercial artist. She was a talented artist who continued to grow in her skills and abilities through the years, and her employment increased her confidence in her capability to support us with her talent. Mother handled life as well as possible for a single parent in the late 50s and early 60s. Although she appeared strong, confident, and determined to build her career without dependence on her mother; she also battled insecurity and a sense of helplessness.

Mother worked hard and managed her two children without much help from her extended family during the school year, but the summer months were hard, and family members opened their homes to my brother and me. We had wonderful times in the country with our cousins, exploring, swimming, and just being kids. I will always be grateful for the kindness these family members showed me.

In Memphis my brother started delivering newspapers, which helped to contribute to the family income. Mother's salary was meager and she had to be creative in earning extra money by taking additional jobs after her regular work hours. My brother and I became latch-key kids before the term became well known. Yet, we still had fun. We watched TV, explored a near-by stadium, and played with our friends. The times were very different then and, in spite of the lack of supervision, we were able to have relatively normal childhoods. However, our Huck Finn freedom soon became a distant memory when our lives took a sudden turn.

While in Memphis Mother continued a relationship with a man she had met in Eupora. He worked for the telephone company and would occasionally visit Mother in Memphis. Initially, Mother shunned his attentions until circumstances made her think about this relationship as being 'a way out.'

One day Mother, who was clever and talented in fixing things, was trying to make our little home more attractive by reupholstering our couch. As she was instructing my brother on how NOT to take a staple out of the fabric of the couch, she shot a staple into her own eye, causing the complete loss of sight in that eye. Here she was, an artist who did not have complete vision. She felt desperate to find an answer to the dilemma of supporting her children with only one functioning eye. Her difficult situation caused her to re-examine her options. Shortly after losing her eye, Mother married the man from Europa, who became my stepfather. While I think my mother probably loved my stepdad when they married, her circumstances certainly played a significant role in her decision to join him with her ready-made family. This decision would mark a radical change in all of our lives.

Memories from Memphis are filled with carefree living and fun times with our young mother playing baseball and other outdoor games with us and the neighborhood kids in the evenings after work. However, soon after Mother remarried, tension and emotional pain ruled the new household. As a child, I was jealous of my mother's new affection and resented being pulled from my comfort zone of known security. We moved to Jackson, Mississippi, where my stepfather was employed by a local telephone provider, having worked his way up from a lineman to an instructor. Dad, as I begrudgingly called him, had graduated from college at the University of Mississippi and went to the Jackson School of Law in the evenings. He was a devout Catholic, but his devotion to his faith did not influence his actions until his later years. Dad was demanding and dominated our small family, our mother in particular. White glove inspections and long hours of cleaning, waxing, and buffing the wood floors in their newly built house were the norm.

Mother felt the pressure of being in the middle between her challenging new spouse and her perplexed children who needed her protection. It was a difficult marriage for my mother and a very hard life for my brother and me during the years we were still in that house. But joy emerged from that time period as a result of the births of my two younger sisters, who were born in

1962 and 1966. They were, and are, dear and precious members of my family. I couldn't love them more if we shared both parents.

As each sister was born, my brother and I saw a change in our family dynamics. While Dad had never really embraced our being part of his family, he began, even more, to increasingly reject my brother and me, obviously impatient for us to turn 18 so we could leave home and go out on our own. We were often told that as soon as we were of age, he wanted us out of the house. Dad wanted only his biological children around him. Therefore, I felt unwanted, and although I was also eager to be separated from this dysfunctional family, Dad's rejection was painful for me, and had a negative impact on me for many years.

Mother was in the middle, but desperate to give her second marriage a chance, not wanting to add another failed marriage to her perceived list of life's mistakes. During our high school years, Mother managed to send my brother and me to live with an aunt for a year in an effort to save her rapidly deteriorating marriage. This 'farming out' of my brother and me broke my heart, as I shamefully saw it as a total rejection. I felt unwanted by my own mother, and my insecurities mounted as I hoped for a new life. I recall that as a teenager, I prayed some of my first prayers while lying in bed with tears drenching my pillow. I cried out to God for a better life than my mom's miserable existence in her, seemingly, tense and loveless marriage. I could not have known how wonderfully God would answer the prayers of my longing heart.

As an adult looking back at my life, I see that the hard work we were required to do in my stepfather's house, although a travesty to my wounded heart, was probably part of what kept my brother and me from getting involved in other, more damaging teenage behavior. My stepfather was inexperienced in his dealings with children at the time, and he definitely made wrong choices in his marital relationship. However, I now have a better understanding of life's realities and see that he was simply a young man trying to fit his own dysfunction into the chaos of his new wife's complicated life, which involved the unfamiliar element of two teenage children. Marriage is difficult even under the best of circumstances. My stepfather did the best he could in light of his own wounds and lack of experience. In later years, my stepfather and I made peace, forgiving one another for the pain we caused each other in those earlier times. After that point, our relationship was congenial and kind until his death in 2007.

As hard as it was on me during that time, the greatest wounds were not to my body, but to my fragile heart. My woundedness eventually drove me to God, who has been able to heal and reframe my memories. Who has not lived with regrets and the pain of wrong choices? As I have experienced God's grace toward me in my own dysfunctional actions and reactions, I can more readily extend it to others who have also injured my heart. Often, I find that my damaged pride is more the issue rather than my difficult circumstances.

My brother graduated from high school in 1967, and in response to my stepfather's wishes that we leave the house after graduating from high school, my brother joined the Navy. The next year, one week after my high school graduation, I left home, feeling like a victim, afraid and insecure, but also determined to escape! I had nowhere to go, so I managed to get some loans and move to the college campus for the summer program at the University of Southern Mississippi. I eventually met and, in 1970, married my life partner. We fell in love and eloped to Livingston, Alabama, to get married. At that time, I did not regret our elopement, knowing that getting married in a beautiful church wedding was impossible for me, a girl without a loving father to give her away, no money, and no family support. It wasn't until after I became a Christian that I regretted we did not make our vows formally before God, asking for His blessing on our union. My desire was realized on our tenth anniversary when my husband surprised me with a lovely church wedding with our friends and church family around us to witness our vows, which we made before God in a small military chapel at Ft. Detrick, Maryland. This gift from my husband was a public acknowledgement and renewal of the private covenant we had made when we first married in the civil ceremony.

Finding a man to marry as wonderful as my husband was another example of God's graciousness. My husband had grown up attending church and came from a praying, Bible believing family. However, by the time we married, he was more of an intellectual believer. He knew the truth, but did not obey it, as evidenced by his marriage to ME - an obvious pagan!

The admonition in Scripture, specifically in **2 Corinthians 6:14,** is to *not be bound together with unbelievers.* The phrase is translated as "unequally yoked" (NKJV), "mismatched with unbelievers" (NRSV), and "Do not try to work together as equals with unbelievers" (TEV) in other versions of the Bible. The Old Testament agricultural illustration refers to using different types of animals in a farmer's yoke. The effectiveness of the combination is diminished by the differences in the strength and pull of the two dissimilar animals. Though the text refers to church matters, it can also be applied in a wider spectrum to alliances in which one side is unequal to the other in focus, goals, and strength, as in a business alliance or intimate relationships, such as in choosing a marriage partner.

I was so wounded by my past and handicapped by my New Age thinking that a true believer should have explained the Gospel to me long before any involvement. We were young and in love and mistakenly thought that we were an invincible duo that could conquer any challenges that life handed us. The loss of our first two unborn children in the earliest years of our marriage showed us that we were not in charge. The live birth of our first-born daughter a few years later made her birth seem so miraculous and prepared me to hear the message of Christ's love and forgiveness. I had to first learn that my naturally endowed hips, which I thought were ideal for bearing children, were actually useless unless God opened the womb and brought the baby to term. I look forward to meeting my first two children in Glory.

After graduation from the University of Southern Mississippi, my husband was accepted into the University of Mississippi Law School. As a result, I quit school after completing two and one half years of academic work, and we moved to Oxford, Mississippi. We both worked hard so he could obtain his law degree. However, in the fourth year of our marriage, and in my husband's last year of law school, God did some wonderful things in our lives. Little did I know what God had in store for us that year! Our first baby was born, a beautiful blue-eyed little girl. When we looked at that lovely little one, perfect in every way, we began to turn our attention toward the God who created such a wonder in so small a package.

As I recall our uncertain beginnings, I am mindful that God had a plan for our lives that we could never even imagine. Shortly after our daughter's birth, we had a visitor who introduced us to the good news of Jesus Christ. Because my husband was in law school, and we needed additional income, we were also managing a small motel, work that enabled me to stay home with our new baby. One afternoon, our friend, Henry, stopped by for a visit. He was very different than we were. We had been watching him because he didn't drink, use foul language, or tell crude and coarse jokes as we, and several of our other friends, did. Henry also went to church and belonged to a Bible study group. That afternoon, he explained the good news of the gospel to us. He said that we were sinners in need of a Savior. Well, that's as far into the conversation as I got. I reasoned that because my husband and our friend were both Protestants, this must be a Protestant problem that our friend was discussing.

My understanding of religion was one of empty rituals, required attendance, and mixed messages that encouraged me to compare my sin with the sins of others. I measured up pretty well against serial killers, adulterers, murderers, and thieves, so I thought I was not as bad. My rule keeping gave me a false sense of security. I respected God, as I understood Him, but had no idea that I too had a sin problem that separated me from a relationship with Him. This was a new and radical thought for me to grasp with my old theological infrastructure, and it simply did not compute. I felt as though I was listening to two athletes discuss intricate game plans that were beyond my understanding and which did not pertain to me.

Because my husband had been raised in a Christian home, he knew what was missing in his life. We got to the end of the conversation with our friend, and my husband and I both prayed a prayer of commitment. I concluded that my husband needed this religious awakening and, as a supportive wife, I wanted to cooperate. I actually thought this was a step in the right direction toward the idealized family I had long desired. I had no understanding as to how our friend's message related to me, but God was faithful to honor my desire to know Him, even without my total understanding of these unfamiliar concepts.

I had never heard the message of Christ's love for me and of His redeeming sacrifice in such personal terms. I understood the crucified Christ died for the sins of the world, but I had not heard that He died for MY sins. Me . . . a sinner?? Saved . . . from what?? Why did I need a Savior?? I had to find out, so I decided to go to the tangible source of the information, our only Bible. This was a huge family Bible (coffee table presentation size) that had been a gift from my husband's two godly aunts. Like the college student I had been, I began reading from this 'Holy Book' with highlighter in hand (much to my husband's horror), voraciously devouring and underlining each new detail I learned. I underlined as I read in the books of Matthew, Mark, Luke, John, and Acts. I could hardly believe that this was a true story. I had some vague knowledge of some of the events in the life of Christ, but most of the information was new to me. Soon, I found out who Jesus is and that He came to *save His people from their sins* (Matt. 1:21). In Luke 9:56, I discovered that He *did not come to destroy men's lives, but to save them.* In Acts 16:31, I learned that I needed to *believe in the name of the Lord Jesus to be saved.* All of this was new, but I began to see that I needed to be saved, not just Protestants like my husband and Henry. As I read the gospels for the first time, my belief system was challenged, but I kept reading. Because I wasn't a Buddhist or a Hindu, I automatically thought I was a Christian with guaranteed entrance into heaven. I mentally aligned myself on the right side, but I didn't understand why it was so important.

Meanwhile, the husband I once knew began to transform into a new man. His language improved markedly and his attitude began to make a positive shift as well. I noticed, but I still didn't understand the God who could, and would, transform a life and change a heart. This was such a personal and interactive relationship with God, which was totally unfathomable to me. However, our God is so gracious. Looking back, I see how patient the Lord was with me. I had prayed a prayer of commitment with the wrong motive, but He saw my willingness to know Him, and He continued to draw me to Himself.

Six months after our friend's visit, I consented to be baptized, taking the 'next' step, but still not quite grasping the personal connection with Jesus Christ. My husband was accepted into the army as a JAG officer after graduation from law school, and I was getting baptized so that I would be able to fit into other churches as my husband and I moved around to the various military communities.

I was nervously watching the woman in the baptism line ahead of me getting baptized. I was captivated by the words the pastor spoke regarding the woman's new commitment to Christ. As he explained what her need was and how Christ met it in the sacrifice of His own life, I began to understand. The enlightenment of comprehension occurred; a spiritual window opened and a fresh breeze blew through the old cobwebs of non-understanding, leaving me with a new and clearer perception of the very words our friend had spoken six months earlier. I had fallen far short of God's holy standard of right living. I had offended God by disobeying His moral absolutes, opposing His will, and attempting to live by my own standards. I was a sinner and my sin separated ME from a relationship with God. The pastor spoke of our new commitment to Christ and how Christ met our needs in the sacrifice of His own life. Jesus willingly suffered and died at the hands of wicked and sinful men, taking the punishment for sin that should have been mine. Because Jesus had never sinned Himself, He was a sinless sacrifice who did not deserve death; therefore, He became my substitute and the sufficient sacrifice for all sin. I deserved death, but Jesus paid not only my sin debt, but also for the sins of all who believe in Him. As a result of His obedience, God raised Jesus from the dead, giving Him the name that is above all names, so that every knee will bow and every tongue will confess that He is Lord.

By His magnificent triumph over death, I could have forgiveness of my sins and eternal life with Him, by just trusting in what He had done. God demonstrated His own love toward me, as the Scripture says, in that, while I was still a sinner, Christ died for me (Rom. 5:8)! The pastor said that we could not make God love us more by going to church or by doing good things. He already loves us just as we are, but we need the blood of Jesus Christ to save us from our willful and sinful ways that deserve His condemnation.

The pastor went on to say that we who were being baptized had been crucified with Christ – as if we too had died! We were being buried in baptism with Him under the water and would be raised up to walk in the newness of life, just as though we too would experience a type of resurrection from being spiritually dead. The proverbial light bulb went on for me. All of a sudden, the words from the big family Bible, our friend, my husband's changed life, and the pastor's words all came together. I finally understood. God's love for me and his preciously extravagant and sacrificial gift of the very lifeblood of His Son, Jesus, were given so generously for ME!

That momentous day in 1974, I made a true commitment to Jesus Christ. I asked Him to forgive me for my rebellion against Him and to cover me with His blood as payment for my sin debt. I fell in love with Him that day, and I have not been the same since. I came up out of that baptismal pool a new creation, and I have never turned back. I was so deficient in my spiritual understanding that God had to bring me up to zero before I even registered on the spiritual growth chart. At that point, I began to take in the Word of God, the Bible, like a vital blood transfusion. It was so new and different for me as I learned of the love the Father had, and still has, for me, a girl without a loving father, at that time. No longer was I rejected, but I was accepted just as I was; no longer did I just have a religion, but I had a true relationship with the Living God. No longer was I a so-called 'happy pagan' – happy on the outside, but wounded and broken on the inside. I was saved!

I would like to be able to report that on that day in 1974, I became perfect, or almost perfect, in every way, but I am unable to do so! It took a while for me to get those spiritual truths deep down inside my heart. It took a long time for my mind to be washed by the renewing of His Word. I had years of lies to address, habits to change, hurts to expose, and wounds to heal. But I had begun to take the first steps on the journey toward healing as a true believer in Jesus Christ. Bit by bit, the Lord addressed, and He continues to address, my sin issues of pride and self-righteousness, and to heal the wounds of my past. He continues to renew my mind with His Word and to thrill my heart with His love. In addition, He grants me the wonderful gift of forgiveness for my daily sins when I stumble and fall. The Scripture teaches me that when I sin or choose to rebel or disregard God's clear will in the Bible, I can be forgiven by simply and humbly coming to God to confess and agree with God that what I did displeased Him. When I honestly confess my sin, I understand that God has forgiven me for that sin and for all the other sins I have committed, even those of which I was unaware (1 John 1:9). His forgiveness and a restored relationship with Him give me a joy that springs from a fresh and intimate relationship with the holy God.

After almost forty years, I still seek to walk in a manner worthy of my high calling. Each morning, I treasure my intimate devotional quiet time with Him. Armed with His authoritative Word, the Bible, I receive direction for my life, ***straight from His Word.***

Mother 1948

Mother on her wedding day, 1948

Dad and Mother, High School Graduation, 1948

III
SNARED BY THE DECEIVER

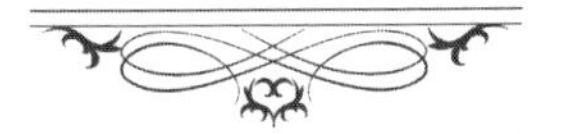

Many gasp in alarm when they see me, but you take me in stride.
Just as each day brims with your beauty, my mouth brims with praise.
Psalm 71:7-8 (TM)

After my brother and I left home, my mother found more freedom as tension lessened without our presence. Mother still had my two little sisters at home, but by age forty-seven, she had managed to complete her Bachelor of Arts degree in Art Education at Mississippi College, a local Christian college. This was a tremendous accomplishment for Mother and a great boost to her self-esteem. She seemed to be released from her dark, insecure feelings about herself and to shake off much of the victim mentality she maintained in her relationships with both my biological father and my stepfather. Mother had always told us that she had barely graduated from high school and did not have any academic abilities. However, with tutoring and babysitting help from her friends, Mother proved that statement incorrect as she triumphantly completed her degree in 1977.

Mother had responsibilities with her two younger children and also with her ailing mother. From time to time, as my grandmother got older, she stayed with my mother, step-father, and my younger sisters. During these years, Grandmother tutored Mother in becoming a more effective trance channeler, conducting séances, and promoting New Age thought. Even when she wasn't in my mother's home, my grandmother and mother had a teacher/student correspondence, with Grandmother commenting on Mother's impressions which were received from her spirit guides. They got along well during that time, as my mother was an eager student.

Grandmother was a hardworking, no nonsense woman who had carried her family of eight through the depression years by employing creative cooking skills. Even as I knew her, nothing was wasted or destroyed if it could be repurposed later. She collected hundreds of recipes, making comments on each one as she entered them into her vast collection. Her smiles were rare, but when they did appear, they were contagious. She died in 1986 at the age of 81. By this time Grandmother had already passed her mantle of spiritism to my mother who was actively pursuing my grandmother's satanic craft after her graduation from college. Of course, Mother did not see it as a 'satanic craft.' At first, she was simply seeking to help her friends with this new ability or talent learned and passed down from my grandmother.

Mother began to embrace her way of life in spiritism just as I was growing in my own relationship with Christ. As I understood more, the divide between us grew wider. We were moving in diametrically opposite directions, and I struggled with how to handle my relationship with Mother. In my 'all or nothing' mentality, I wanted both a relationship with my mother and also with Christ. My heart wanted to please my mother, but my faith was in total conflict. I had to choose between following Christ and re-embracing the old ways. I chose Christ and left family and friends in order to follow Him. I renounced and rejected all of my grandmother's teachings since I was growing more and more familiar with the great division between these two ways of life. I knew the difference between spiritual darkness and spiritual light and would not return to the darkness. Spiritual darkness can actually be physically perceived and the light is equally real, influencing both thoughts and attitudes. I did not want to return to that foreboding spiritual oppression.

My relationship with Mother continued to grow more difficult as time went by. As the subject matter of our discussions touched on religion or spiritual topics, we disagreed sometimes heatedly, but on other more superficial issues, we got along well. I later determined that I could not convince or persuade Mother to change her convictions, but I could love her unconditionally in the same way that Jesus loved her. Love and acceptance are the evidence of true Christianity, and I hoped it would be an irresistible magnet (John 13:34-35; 15:12, 17).

As I look back, I could have been even more loving to Mother, more Christ-like. Unfortunately, life is full of regrets. When I was in her home, I felt I was battling for my own life in Christ. The spiritual warfare was intense. The mere appearance of my Bible set Mother on edge. She was volatile and quick to erupt into a disagreement, if I was not careful to resist the bait. Her seemingly non-judgmental attitude and acceptance regarding many other matters did not extend to my faith or to me! She was intolerant of my views, as much as I was of her views. Also, my own fears were heightened as I fought to keep the truth in the minds of my two young daughters, and to protect them from the deception of the enemy. At the same time, I so desperately wanted to share the truth about Christ with my mother. I was torn between moving forward, braving the dragons in an offensive posture, or holding back in a defensive mode protecting my daughters from the deceptions and distortions of the truth.

Mother had her own family responsibilities, as well as her professional ones. During the latter years of my grandmother's life, she accelerated her tutoring of Mother, seemingly getting her pupil ready to 'take over.' By the time my grandmother died, she had passed down her 'faith,' and truly, her deception to her daughter. Ironically, I too desired to pass down my own faith to my daughters; but oh, what a difference between the everlasting and inexhaustible love of God and the temporal satisfaction of such ungodly influences!

As Mother embraced her new mantle, her reputation and fame increased in her local area. She was often interviewed on the radio and featured in newspaper articles, especially around Halloween. The majority of Mother's predictions, according to her, were correct in what she shared with others, regarding their pasts and their relationships with their loved ones. She was very proud of her accuracy and felt that her skill was validated by the responses of her clients. Deuteronomy 18:21-22 states that a prophet who claims to speak for the Lord must be 100% correct because he represents the Lord God. However, people were drawn to Mother's genuine concern for them, as well as her kindness. She listened well, and people loved her acceptance of them, her non-judgmental attitude, and her open door policy. Mother was approachable, and she always enjoyed laughing with her friends and clients. Mother would actually do almost anything to help another person: give money, expend time and attention for their needs, and/or provide a sanctuary for them during difficult times. My stepfather was not totally pleased with these traits, but they lived somewhat separate lives, and he gradually grew to tolerate her friends and idiosyncrasies, and later, to even admire them as she received public acclaim.

Though Mother taught a lie and led others astray, I do not believe Mother knowingly or intentionally sought to deceive anyone. She too was deceived by the enemy of her soul and led others into the same deception. For the most part, Mother was kind-hearted and tried to help others by offering her skills to comfort them. Although we talked about the source of her information, Mother denied that it was from Satan. She was adamant that her spirit guides were of God and that even Jesus represented Himself, masked as one of her guides, called Samuel. When a new book, *The Course in Miracles,*[10] came on the market in 1975, Mother quickly embraced it and brought others into her way of thinking through the classes she taught using it as the text. My heart is so heavy to think that Mother was so misguided. Even today, I tremble when I hear about well-meaning Christians channeling non-Scriptural words to others from a so-called 'Jesus'! They too are deceived.

As the years passed, my mother became a great devotee of *The Course in Miracles.* The book, originally in three volumes, was 'scribed' or channeled by Helen Schucman between the years of 1965 and 1972. Schucman (1910-1981) was a clinical and research psychologist, an avowed atheist, and ethnical Jew with a mixed bag of religious dabblings in Catholicism and Protestantism, though she remained a professing atheist for the majority of her life. Her colleague, William Thetford (1923-1988), introduced

10 Schucman, Helen. *A Course in Miracles: Text, Workbook for Students, Manual for Teachers.* New York: Foundation for Inner Peace, 1996.

her to the form of meditation that later produced *The Course in Miracles.* At Thetford's suggestion, Schucman began recording her encounters and on October 21, 1965, she claims that her voice told her, "This is a course in miracles. Please take notes." [11]

Is this book indeed dictated by Jesus or is it from some other source? If it were from the real Jesus, it would have to be consistent with the Scriptures and teach the same message of reconciliation with God through the atoning blood of Jesus Christ. But the leaders of *The Foundation for a Course in Miracles* and those close to the channeler, Helen Schucman, are clear that their teachings are not in line with biblical Christianity. Instead, they use biblical terminology to express their metaphysical and Gnostic philosophy, and teach "that we are all equally Christ"[12]. Dean Halverson, a Researcher for *Spiritual Counterfeits Project Journal,* states:

> (*The Course)* has also found a ready and expanding audience within the Christian Church, which is not surprising either. Biblical illiteracy is rampant and commitment to orthodoxy often less than vigorous and sometimes consciously absent. Those conditions are aggravated by the very nature of the Course writings. Couched in biblical terminology and allegedly dictated by Jesus Christ, they easily confuse and seem designed specifically for that purpose.[13]

There is no doubt that these teachings are incompatible with Christianity. Even the founder of *The Foundation for a Course in Miracles,* Kenneth Wapnick, who is also the editor of the channeled material and author of several books expounding on *The Course in Miracles,* does not mince words as he declares:

> *The Course* is not compatible with biblical Christianity. There are three basic reasons. One is the Course's idea that God did not create the world. The second is the Course's teaching that Jesus was not the only Son

[11] Gale Group, Inc. *Encyclopedia of Occultism and Parapsychology,* "Helen Schucman." n pag. Web. 7 May 2013.

[12] Halverson, Dean C. "A Matter of Course: Conversation with Kenneth Wapnick." *Spiritual Counterfeits Project Journal.* Vol. 7.1. 1987. 12.

[13] Halverson 9.

> of God. The third involves the Course's assertion that Jesus did not suffer and die for our sins.[14]

In the Introduction to *A Course in Miracles* it states: "*A Course in Miracles* was 'scribed' by Dr. Helen Schucman through a process of inner dictation she identified as coming from Jesus."[15] Though the text is purported to be dictated by 'Jesus,' this 'Jesus' does not insist on the same Christian standard of exclusivity found in the Bible. The biblical Jesus clearly states: "I am the way, the truth and the life. No one comes to the Father but through Me" (John 14:6). This new 'Jesus' of *A Course in Miracles* is inclusive of all forms of religious teaching. In fact, the Course material also states:

> Although Christian in statement, the Course deals with universal spiritual themes. It emphasizes that it is but one version of the universal curriculum. There are many others, this one differing from them only in form. They all lead to God in the end.[16]

This philosophy of Universalism espouses that at some point all people will be saved and go to heaven. Probe Ministries is in the forefront of Christian apologetics and explains Universalism:

> Routinely (the Universalist) views stray from orthodox Christian belief and away from the Bible. In numerous places the Bible refers to a time of judgment where the righteous are granted eternal life and the wicked are given over to eternal punishment (cf. Matthew 25:31-46, Luke 16:19-31, Revelation 20:11-15). Furthermore, Jesus, as well as the New Testament writers, referred to a place of eternal punishment (cf. Matthew 5:22, 18:8-9, Mark 9:43, 48, Revelation 19:20, 20:10, etc.). The Bible is very emphatic regarding the doctrine of eternal punishment. Universalism rejects this teaching and replaces it with its own.[17]

---

[14] Halverson 10.

[15] Schucman An Introduction.

[16] Schucman An Introduction, What It Is.

[17] Holmes, Ryan. "What is Your Position on Universalism?" Probe Ministries 2007: n pag. Web. 19 February 2013.

It is evident that this new 'Jesus' is not the biblical Jesus of the Scriptures.

Though there is little doubt that *The Course in Miracles* is not a Christian text, there are other questionable books whose titles portray them as being more closely aligned with Christian/ biblical concepts. *The Course in Miracles* is also not the only text thought to be dictated by Jesus. Two of these books with which I am familiar use alluring and similar titles to entice the reader to believe that God or Jesus is talking directly to the readers through the authors. I was personally deceived by one of these books, and am writing my book to warn readers about the dangers of other books of this nature.

After Mother's death, my sister and I discovered stacks of letters that Mother had saved from her correspondence with my grandmother. The letters were written by Mother and were returned to her with notes and comments from Grandmother. In one of the letters written in 1973, Mother states that she feels there is a spiritual battle going on within her with "God and Jesus on one side and my angels on the other side." Later she states that she is convinced that her "angels" are good, and then begins to fully embrace my Grandmother's teachings. During that period, Mother was in college and had taken a Bible class. The fact that she knew enough to place God and Jesus on an opposing side from her familiar spirits reveals a budding insight. But what was recognizable and comfortable for her triumphed in this early, internal battle between light and darkness. The Scriptures warn about the enemy of our souls appearing as an angel of light in 2 Corinthians 11:14, *No wonder, for even Satan disguises himself as an angel of light.* This marked a turning point in Mom's belief system. She actively chose the darkness rather than the light of Christ.

IV
MY DETOUR

My enemies are talking behind my back, watching for their chance to knife me.
The gossip is: "God has abandoned him. Pounce on
him now; no one will help him."
Psalm 71:10–11 (TM)

For approximately two and one half years in the early 1980s, I too fell for the deception found in a similar book to *The Course in Miracles.* But God did not leave me there. As Mother was taking her mantle from my grandmother, I was undergoing a deeper struggle for my heart. I naively thought that books that spoke about God or devotion to God were Christian books that might have something contained within that would help me grow in my relationship with God. In the same way after my baptism, as I stood at the front of the Protestant church and shook hands with the church members, I had naively assumed that all who were there had also fallen in love with Jesus in the same way I had just experienced. In my guilelessness, I asked many of the older church members, "How long have you known Him?" and "How long have you loved Him?" as they were shaking my hand after the service. I am sure my questions shocked the elderly members of the congregation, but I was experiencing the first blush of newly discovered love. This innocence concerning Christian spiritual matters set me up for the detour in my Christian walk. I did not expect in my fleeing from spiritism that I would run directly into it in Christian circles. Christian words were wrapped around New Age practices and I blindly swallowed the lie that this was devotion to God.

The snare that entrapped me early in my Christian journey was a popular devotional book that is still read today by many

Christians, entitled *God Calling.*[18] I began to use it in my morning devotions. I had already come to the understanding that spiritism was not of God, and I had renounced all from that genre that I had accepted before trusting in Christ. Unfortunately, it is not as though I had a clear box of heresy to dump and be done with, but rather as God brought things to light in my understanding, I quickly labeled the wrong thinking and rejected it. It was a process - not a one-time event.

I had been a Christian for approximately six years and enjoyed a rich fellowship with the Lord. I was constantly hungry for the Word of God and spent the majority of my spare time, either studying or reading the Bible. I had much to learn and found that the Word of God provided an endless supply of godly behavior for me to emulate as I was removing the old ways. I longed to be a Bible teacher, so I began to prepare. My exposure to Kay Arthur of Precept Ministries had left an indelible mark on my heart, as I too longed to teach God's Word. As a busy young mother of two (Beka, born in 1974, and Kay, born in 1976), I wanted to use my time to grow in my knowledge of God.

I had received a copy of *God Calling* and had read the introduction about how two women sat down and began to "listen" to God and had written down what they heard. I yearned, and even now continue to desire an intimate relationship with God. That has not changed in my life, but the way I seek Him has changed. At that time, I thought that I could imitate what the listeners had done. I did not see any conflict in the procedure because the Scriptures contain many outright conversations that God had with a variety of persons. I reasoned that He would or could speak to me too. I knew of no prohibition in attempting this experiment.

Since becoming a Christian, I have maintained a personal daily journal. I love to copy God's words from the Bible and comment on how I perceive their application to me. Many of my journal entries are a recap of the day before with praise, thanksgivings, confessions, and written prayers regarding what

[18] Russell, A.J., ed. *God Calling.* Uhrichsville, OH: Barbour Publishing, Inc., 1989.

concerns me for the day, and an application of God's Word from my consistent reading of the Scriptures. When I began my journal, I would frequently re-read what I had written for my own encouragement, seeing how God had answered prayer and how loving His words were from the Scriptures. I needed that faith building encouragement as I was growing in my understanding of this great God in whom I had put my trust.

However, after considering the book, *God Calling*, I added an opportunity for God to speak directly to me, as was exampled in that text. I would get quiet on the inside and listen for God to speak, always with the understanding that if anything conflicted with the written Word of God, it would not be God speaking, but my own inner thoughts. I would write the first things that would come to my mind, which I called 'the voice of the Lord.' Most of what I heard, in retrospect, was self-centered and humanistic. I did not get specific direction for my issues, but what I did get were words that pumped up my ego and pointed to the good of mankind. I wrote down everything I heard.

As time went on, I realized that I was the only Christian I knew who was sitting before the Lord in the same manner I did. I wondered if this was really 'of God.' Still I continued my journals. During this time, I experienced the most difficult test to my marriage. Although I did not realize it at the time, there was a subtle temptation to turn from the God of the Bible in order to pursue my own desires. This journaling technique grew for me, and each day, I would be diligent to wake up at 5 a.m. to have my time in the Word and with the 'voice of the Lord.' Gradually, the 'voice of the Lord' began to monopolize my devotional time. Sadly, I did not see the harm in this practice, but something must have worried me about it because I kept asking God to tell me if this was truly His method of communicating with me.

My deceptive pursuit of God went on for a few years. We moved to Atlanta with the military, and because of my confusion, I attempted to call Charles Stanley, the well-known Pastor of the First Baptist Church of Atlanta. He was a man I trusted and respected through having viewed his televised services, and I thought he would be able to tell me if this practice was of God.

Now, I can laugh when I think of how skilled his secretary was at guiding me toward other church counselors. I hung up the phone, not angry or feeling rejected, but rather understanding what a busy man Dr. Stanley was. I wasn't interested in talking with a stranger of whom I knew nothing, and counseling was foreign to me at that time, so I closed the door on that avenue of inquiry. I am thankful though that God did not give me an easy answer, or I might not even be writing this book today. The struggle made the answer and the response clearly mine.

Gradually, the Lord led me to see some similarities in what the women in *God Calling* were doing, and a spiritist séance. These 'anonymous listeners' spoke of God, but they were not seeking the living God through His Word, and these new words that they heard superseded the Bible itself as a latter day revelation. They felt their dictated word was fresher, clearer, and more valid than God's written word from the Bible. I also came across some information on *automatic writing* and with that, my eyes were opened! Automatic writing, often associated with the Ouija Board, is a technique by which the subject is guided by another entity to communicate psychic messages. These messages are written down without the conscious thought of the writer, or in the case of the Quija Board are 'guided' messages. This was what I was calling the 'voice of the Lord!' Once I was able to mentally remove *God Calling* from the Christian genre, I began to see more similarities to my Spiritualist background.

Since conducting more research for this book, I have discovered that even the spiritists caution against using the Ouija Board and automatic writing. Several psychics mentioned in John Ankerberg and John Weldon's *Encyclopedia of New Age Beliefs* have also warned against the use of this technique:

> . . . even seasoned occultists and psychic researchers warn against using the Ouija Board. **Medium Edgar Cayce** himself called it "dangerous." Edmund Gruss refers to **medium Donald Page**, an "exorcist" of the "Christian" Spiritualist Church, who asserts that "the majority of possession cases" result from involvement with the Ouija Board. Page believes it is one of the quickest and easiest ways there is to become possessed.

Discussing the relation of Ouija Boards to automatic writing, **psychic researcher Martin Ebon** also alleges that possession is a frequent occurrence: It is common that people who get into this sort of game think of themselves as having been "chosen" for a special task. The Ouija Board will often say so, either directly or by implication. It may speak of "tests" that the sitters must undergo to show that they are "worthy" of this otherworldly attention. I have not been able to figure out why this is so, but quite often the Ouija turns vulgar, abusive or threatening. It grows demanding and hostile, and sitters may find themselves using the board or automatic writing compulsively, as if "possessed" by a spirit, or hearing voices that control and command them. This is no longer rare. I'd say it is now so frequent as to be common.

Psychic Alan Vaughan also points out the following information, "It is significant, however, that the greatest outcry against the use of Ouijas has come from the Spiritualists not the parapsychologists. In England, Spiritualist groups are petitioning to ban the sale of Ouijas as toys for children–not because of vague dangers of 'unhealthy effects on naive, suggestible persons'–but because they fear that the children will become possessed".

Psychic/spiritist Harold Sherman, president of ESP Research Associates Foundation in Little Rock, Arkansas, agrees: "The majority who have become involved with possessive and other entities came by this experience through the Ouija Board". The irony however, is that, despite the warnings, most people continue to view the Ouija Board as a harmless pastime . . .[19]

As my eyes opened, I was appalled at how long I had been mired in that pit of deception. However, forsaking this cultic

[19] Ankerberg, John and John Weldon, *Encyclopedia of New Age Beliefs*. Eugene, OR: Harvest House, 1996, 152-153.

practice was harder than I expected. I found that it was like a drug to which I had become addicted. My mind screamed to return to the 'voice.' I struggled for weeks to pull away. My emotions were unpredictable and I experienced great inner turmoil! The voice I heard very clearly during this time was one that constantly condemned me, and then at other times it was like a siren call from Greek mythology, as the sea nymphs attempted to lure unsuspecting sailors to destruction on the rocks surrounding their island. The voice repeatedly bid me to return to the sweet intimacy of the 'voice.' On one hand, the persistent accusations of my past sins were the whips the enemy used to flagellate and shame me. On the other hand, the siren call exposed my longing for intimacy. Again, my eyes were opening even more as I realized the true 'voice of the Lord' is not one of continual and undeserved condemnation or of the extremes I was experiencing. God's words through the Scriptures did not contain the same harshness I was hearing, so I began to do some research.

I began to study the 'sound' of God's voice from the Bible, and saw that condemnation and shame were not a part of His loving communication with His people who have been saved by grace. I composed a chart so that I could better evaluate the voice I heard. I no longer wanted to be the game piece with which the enemy of my soul sported. Jesus had forgiven my sin, even the GUILT of my sin and one can no longer be guilty of that which is forgiven. He had washed me whiter than snow. My sin was atoned for at the cross by the blood of Jesus Christ. He had cast my sin as far away as the east is from the west when I asked His forgiveness, trusted in His atonement, and surrendered my life to Him. My God was not bringing those sins up again – He had dismissed them! It was my enemy who taunted me with my failures. This influence was not of God! Even though my failings were real, I could quickly point my accuser to my Advocate, Jesus Christ, who paid my sin debt in full.

As my comprehension increased, one of the first things I did was to burn my old journals. I was so ashamed and embarrassed that I had been snared by this adversary who was seeking to reel me in to practice what my mother had been doing for years. I did not ever want my children, or anyone else, to discover my old journal notes; so after confessing my sin before God and sharing an understanding of what had almost happened to me with my immediate family, we sat around the fireplace and burned all of my journal notes from those previous years. I renounced what I called the 'voice of the Lord' and began to experience greater freedom in my walk with God. This was all a part of my breaking free from this 'voice of the Lord.' John 8:32 states, "You will know the truth and the truth will make you free." I still journal, but now I focus more on God's Word, and I still read devotionals, but only from those with a clear Christian testimony.

I have since found out that *God Calling* is not even considered to be a Christian book by those who have studied the New Age movement, and it is also linked with other New Age books such as *The Course in Miracles.* This was an eye-opener for me. The irony of it is that although I was rejecting my mother's way of life, Satan, the one who often comes to us disguised as an angel of light, had dressed spiritism up to look like devotion to God. It shocked me to see that I was using the same method of spiritual communication as my mother, only with a pseudo-Christian covering. I made up my mind from that time forward to study and memorize the Word of God...to focus on it and to recognize His communication to me through His written Word.

Many believers are still drawn to *God Calling* and a subsequent book, *Jesus Calling* (a book I will discuss in more detail later), saying that the books have helped them through difficult times with the inspiring words of affirmation. The Bible, which is quoted in both books, though often out of context, has the power to bless others when it is read. However, Scripture is frequently quoted in cultic literature, as even *The Course in Miracles* attests. Therefore, the use of Scripture does not validate Christian content. Please understand that as I discuss these books, I am not judging the hearts of these authors, only the process they used in scribing their works and the contents of their writings.

The allure of these books is real. After all, who wouldn't want to hear a personal message from God Himself? But many readers are unaware of the dubious origins of these manuscripts. *God*

Calling was written anonymously in the early 1930s, and was edited by A.J. Russell, who was an advocate for the form of guidance the two listeners practiced. When Russell's own book, *For Sinners Only,* was published earlier, it was denounced by Christians as "deplorable and dangerous." [20] Yet, *God Calling* practiced the same techniques Russell espoused and was more readily received.

A.J. Russel states in his introduction to *God Calling*:

> Not one woman, but two have written this book; and they seek no praise. They have elected to remain anonymous and to be called "Two Listeners." But the claim which they make is an astonishing one, that **their message has been given to them, today, here in England, by the Living Christ Himself.** . . None could have written this book unless he or she was a Christian and in touch with the Living Founder of Christianity.[21]

As the Two Listeners utilized the technique of automatic writing that Russell encouraged, one listener evaluated her experience in the Introduction of *God Calling*:

> From the first, beautiful messages were given to her [the other listener] by our Lord Himself, and every day from then these messages have never failed us. We felt all unworthy and overwhelmed by the wonder of it, and could hardly realize that *we* **were being taught, trained and encouraged day by day by HIM personally, when millions of souls, far worthier, had to be content with guidance from the Bible, sermons, their Churches, books and other sources. . . . So to us this book, which we believe has been guided by our Lord Himself, is no ordinary book.**[22]

Russell was a member of The Oxford Group, which promoted this guidance under his leadership. One of Russell's former members, Evangelical Pastor Harold T. Commins, offered his

---

[20] Gruss, Edmond C. "A Summary Critique: God Calling." *Christian Research Journal* 11-01.

[21] Russell Introduction.

[22] Russell Introduction, The Voice Divine.

assessment in Edmond Gruss' article, "A Summary Critique: God Calling":

> Finally, their idea of "guidance" is false to the Scriptures....Sitting down with paper and pencil in hand and letting the mind go absolutely blank and then writing down whatever flashes across the mind as God's orders for the day is beyond anything promised or sanctioned in Scripture. Indeed this "passivity" of mind is a very perilous condition to be in for it is precisely at such moments that Satan gains control and does his devilish work.[23]

If the perceived source of the material does not shock and convince you of the dangers contained in the book, let me produce evidence of theological errors. *God Calling* has many issues in conflict with Christianity. It has been closely examined through the years. Edmond Gruss has a quick list of some of the errors found in *God Calling*. The first three references are evidence of taking Scripture out of context and giving it a new meaning. Gruss's explanation follows the entry. The later selections are additional words that are not represented in the Scriptures, words that add to the Word of God. To make it easier for you to find these selections, I have provided the devotional entry date.

> "When the Bible says, 'God has purer eyes to behold evil,' it means to impute evil in His people. He always sees the good in people..." (p.50) [March 4]. This portion of Habakkuk 1:13 is clearly understood when the rest of the verse is read: God's holiness cannot regard evil with complacency or tolerate it.

> "Remember now abideth these three, Faith, Hope and Charity....Hope, which is confidence in yourself to succeed" (p.110) [June 27]. Titus 1:2 explains that hope is not in self but in God, who can be trusted to carry out His promises.

---

23 Gruss

> "I and my Father are one. One in desire to do good" (p.152) [Sept. 20]. The first sentence is a direct quote from John 10:30. It is followed by an interpretation often given by cults in their rejection of the deity of Christ.

Then there are the statements attributed to Christ that do not borrow from scripture:

> "I need you more than you need me" (p. 60). [March 29]

> "I await the commands of my children" (p. 63). [April 3]

> "Looking to Me all your thoughts are God-inspired. Act on them and you will be led on." [June 13]

> "See Me in the dull, the uninteresting, the sinful, the critical, the miserable." [June 30]

> "I do not delay My second coming. My followers delay it" (p. 177). [Nov. 5]

> "Remember this beautiful Earth on which you are was once only a thought of Divine Mind" (p. 201). [Dec. 18]

> "Wherever the soul is, I am. Man has rarely understood this. I am actually at the center of every man's being, but, distracted with the things of the sense-life, he finds Me not" (p. 55). [March 16]

> "Love is God. Give them love, and you give them God" (p. 72). [April 18]

> "How often mortals rush to earthly friends who can serve them in so limited a way, when the friends who

> are freed from the limitations of humanity [i.e., the dead] can serve them so much better, understand better, protect better, plan better, and even plead better their cause with Me" (p. 145). [Sept. 6]
>
> "Yes! But remember the first hail must be that of the Magi in the Bethlehem stable" (p. 204). [Dec. 24]
>
> "Christ" slips up on this last one. Matthew 2:9-11 indicates that the Magi arrived at Bethlehem a considerable time after Jesus was born. Note that verse 11 mentions their being at the "house." The Magi never did visit Jesus at the stable, but the shepherds did (Luke 2:1 5-20).[24]

Dr. Ankerberg summarizes the teachings contained in *God Calling*:

> The text also denies the atonement (pp. 157, 216), subtly encourages psychic development and spiritistic inspiration under the guise of Christ's personal guidance (pp. 44-45, 55-56, 117-18, 203, 207-08, 214), and often misinterprets Scripture (p. 56).[25] [26]

As I was breaking free from 'the voice,' I decided that I would concentrate actively on the Word of God. I began to study it more earnestly, and also to memorize it. I knew that God said meditating on His Word pleased Him (Ps. 1:1-3), so I learned what meditation was. To the New Ager, meditation is to empty one's mind of everything, to become passive, and to let externally generated thoughts flood the mind, as in my 'voice of the Lord' procedure. In that passive state, the channeler would invite his/her spirit guide to enter the body and direct his/her speech or writing. For the Christian, there is no 'passive state of mind.' Just the opposite! Meditation for the Christian is very

---

[24] Gruss.

[25] Ankerberg 103

[26] The edition cited is: Russell, A.J. *God Calling*. New York: Dodd, Mead and Co., 1945.

brain active, not 'brain-dead.' The Christian meditates by taking Scripture and turning it over in the mind, asking questions, employing a proper method of interpretation, and personalizing the words of Scripture in a prayer back to the Lord. This process is very different from New Age meditation.

Thus began my renewed ardor for the Word of God. It was my insurance against the traps the enemy had set for me in the past, and it fit me for daily life with God, building and establishing my faith and practice. Today, everything in my life continues to be evaluated in light of the Word of God. It has been over 39 years since I met Jesus Christ, and I am still proclaiming the excellencies of Him who called me out of darkness into His marvelous light.

The words of an old Bill and Gloria Gaither song – say it best for me…

Something beautiful, something good;
all my confusion He understood.
All I had to offer Him was brokenness and strife,
but He made – and continues to make – *something beautiful of my life.*[27]

[27] Gaither, Bill and Gloria. "Something Beautiful." Word Publishing, 1971.

WHOSE VOICE DO I HEAR?

In order to view life's emergencies and urgencies with a steady eye and untroubled heart, we must know whether their source is in the mind of the Almighty or in the machination of Abaddon, the destroying spirit of darkness.

V. Raymond Edman

ENEMY'S VOICE	GOD'S VOICE
Berates for blunders	Speaks of the blood that washes white as snow (Is 1:18, 1 Jn 1:9)
Points constantly to sin and condemnation (Rm 8:1)	Convicts, not overlooking sin, but pointing to the Savior (Jn 16:7-15)
TRANSGRESSIONS DEPRESS	**CONFESSION RELEASES** (Ps 32:1-5)
Directs toward self, physical need, social position, self-preservation (Mt 4:3, 8; 16:23-26)	Points to self-denial/selfless service/humility (Rm 8:2-8, 12,13)
Persuades with what we want, what we deserve, what is our right, and what we can do	Points to what we need/what we can do for others (Jn 12:24, Mt 6:8; 1 Jn 3:17)
Flesh **ALWAYS** wants to be seen and heard	Creates a willingness to be unknown/unseen in service to the Lord (Mt 6:1-6)
Leads to self-pity making us sullen, besmirching God's reputation saying, *God is not able*!	Encourages a complete surrender that makes us content in ALL circumstances (Phil 4:11, 12)
Increases sensitivity to imagined slights and dwells on injuries from others until ineffective	Requires obedience which makes us strong (Jn 14:15, 21; Lk 22:25-30)
Torments with the remembrance of past mistakes, heartaches and failures	Urges forgiveness/forgetting what lies behind/pressing on to what lies ahead (Phil 3:13,14)
Delights in taunting weaknesses/ magnifying fears	Reminds of His power in weakness (2 Cor 12:9,10)

ENEMY'S VOICE	GOD'S VOICE
Drives toward rule following, the world's philosophy, empty deception, traditions of men, self-abasement, worship of angels, focus on visions, being inflated without cause, having an independent spirit (Ga 3:10, Col 2:9, 10)	Exalts the Lord's present help/ motivates trust (Ps 46:1; Pv 3:5,6) Shepherds toward freedom in Christ/walking in the Spirit (Gal 5:1, 16)
Tempts with immediate gain at any cost	Tells of eternal gain worth the wait (Rm 5:3-5; Ja 1:2-5)
Magnifies problems as hopeless/ impossible	Reminds of promises to take care of us (Jer 29:11; 32:17; Heb 13:5,6)
Encourages walking by sight/ worldly wisdom (Ps 1:1)	Encourages a walk by faith using Godly wisdom (Ja 3: 13-18; Heb 11:1, 6; Rm 4:16-21)
Sees hosts of evil; points to the nails and thorns	Sees the Captain of the Hosts, the triumph of Calvary's tree (2 Kgs 6:15-17)
Condemns for displays of devotion (2 Sm 6:12-23)	Delights in our open, genuine, transparent love for the Savior
Encourages grumbling/complaining (Nm 11:1)	Rejoices in simple devotion to Jesus Christ/building others up in love (2 Cor 11:3; Rm 9:1)
Delights in knowledge accumulation without application (Rm 9:1)	Promotes obedience to the Word, rather than merely hearing it (Ja 1:22)
The tone is harsh, demanding, and rushing to action	The tone is loving and kind, full of peace and without hurry (Ja 3:13-18; 1 Cor 13)
All self-effort	**All Him (Phil 4:13)**

Chart adapted from *The Disciplines of Life* by V. Raymond Edman, copyright 1948, Scripture Press

V
A MIRACLE OF FORGIVENESS

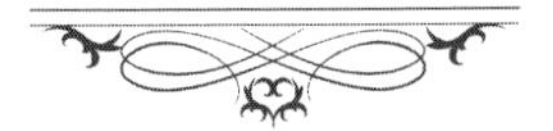

God, you've done it all! Who is quite like You?
Psalm 71:19 (TM)

Before I continue with my story, I feel at this point I must define what I mean when I use the term *miracle.* Earlier, I have referred to the beginning of miraculous things in my life, the miracle of my first live birth, and other wonderful happenings including my finding Jesus as my Lord and Savior! I do not use the term lightly.

A miracle is *a divine act by which God reveals himself to people.*[28]

In Scripture the element of faith is crucial; a natural approach cannot prove or disprove the presence of "miracle." The timing and content of the process can be miraculous, even though the event may seem natural. The revelatory significance is also important. In every case God performed the miracle not merely as a "wonder" to inspire awe but as a "sign" to draw people to himself.[29]

MIRACLES, SIGNS, WONDERS: *Events which unmistakably involve an immediate and powerful action of God designed to reveal His character or purposes. Words used in the Scriptures to describe the miraculous include sign, wonder, work, mighty work, portent, power. These point out the inspired authors' sense of God's pervasive activity in nature, history, and people.*[30]

---

[28] Elwell, Walter A. and Philip W. Comfort. *Tyndale Bible Dictionary*, Tyndale reference library. Wheaton, Ill.: Tyndale House Publishers, 2001. 899.

[29] Elwell 899-900.

[30] Brand, Chad, Charles Draper, Archie England, Steve Bond, E. Ray Clendenen, Trent C. Butler and Bill Latta. *Holman Illustrated Bible Dictionary*. Nashville, TN: Holman Bible Publishers, 2003. 1135.

Miracles documented in the Bible are supernatural occurrences of God's sovereign actions that are marvelously designed to manifest His character or divine purposes to His people. Most often they violate the natural order, or even use the chronology of the natural order God has set in place, to bring the observers to a shock and awe state of worship or realization, as in the plagues on Egypt and the parting of the Red Sea, or Jesus' walking on water, or His turning water to wine. These miracles are divine acts and special interventions by God to reveal Himself through His power to both believers and non-believers. I use the term to describe some event or happening that only God could have accomplished, whether in the timing of His plan, bringing people together for a significant event, or even in transforming the heart and mind of another. These types of miracles are the occurrences where God has revealed His mighty power and love to me, personally and intimately. He is the originator of the display of His power and He is the One who receives all of the glory for the event. Though He may have used others in His plan, He executed it in such a way that only He could have accomplished the work. After the event, I am left in worshipful awe of the God of Love who acted on my behalf, or on the behalf of those I love, to answer my prayers and to reveal His great power. These events are seen with the eye of faith and responded to in love for the God who acts on behalf of His people.

Conversely, *The Course in Miracles*, the book my mother followed, is not about true miracles from God, but rather is spiritistic writing received by an atheist through channeling. The goal of this teaching is to reprogram Christian thinkers to reflect the attitudes and philosophies of New Age and Hindu beliefs. The 'miracles' in this movement are the changes in thought regarding one's worldview.[31] As you can see, this is very different from the miracles I described above.

Even though my early life was dysfunctional with a medium-in-training, single mother who was trying to raise two children without any significant input, any resources, or any contact from

[31] Ankerberg 1-2.

the father of her children, I thought I was secure in the fact that my mother and my grandmother were going to be *there* for my brother and me. When I think back on those years, I am saddened that we considered that concept as *security*! On the other hand, we were well aware that there was a void concerning our biological father. As a result of the bitter divorce and the ensuing separation caused by our living on opposite sides of the country, we grew up without knowing our natural father, and even felt all right about the lack of that relationship. It appeared to us that our parents' decision to divorce was a good one, and we accepted it without question.

After Mother remarried, my brother and I unofficially took the last name of our stepfather to simplify matters at school. We were never adopted, so when the time came for my brother to choose a legal, reliable surname for enlistment into the Navy, as well as for his pending marriage, he decided to finally seek out and meet our father. He was 18 when they met in 1968. After the meeting, although the family resemblance was remarkable, my brother concluded that our father was no different than any other stranger or casual acquaintance. Ultimately, he chose to legally change his name, rejecting our biological father's name and, thus, embracing our stepfather's name and heritage.

I had no such need to formalize my own appellation, especially after I had married and had taken my husband's surname, and I continued to feel apathy regarding my paternal parentage. Mother's bitterness toward my father convinced me that I wanted no part of a man who would reject my mother and her two young children. That is, until Christ began to change my life. As I grew in my understanding of forgiveness, of how much I desperately needed it myself, God decided to challenge the roots of my new found faith.

My biological father and, by now, his wife, kept in touch with my brother during the ensuing years through Christmas cards. During Christmas of 1979, my young family of four visited my brother and his family. As I glanced at the Christmas cards over their fireplace, my brother called my attention to the card from our biological father and his wife. As I read the card, I knew God was asking me to do something that I was not sure I could do. The personal note on the card said, "We hope you find the same peace and joy we have found through Jesus Christ. PTL!" [*Praise the Lord*] My eyes grew wide as I realized that my father was a Christian and now considered my 'brother' in the Lord! I knew that as the Scriptures say in Ephesians, we were one in Christ and that I needed to seek reconciliation! And of course, I also needed to forgive him.

Ephesians 4: 1-6 *Therefore I, the prisoner of the Lord, implore you to walk in a manner worthy of the calling with which you have been called, with all humility and gentleness, with patience,* ***showing tolerance for one another in love, being diligent to preserve the unity of the Spirit in the bond of peace. There is one body and one Spirit, just as also you were called in one hope of your calling; one Lord, one faith, one baptism, one God and Father of all who is over all and through all and in all.***

Romans 12: 17-18 *Never pay back evil for evil to anyone. Respect what is right in the sight of all men. If possible,* ***so far as it depends on you, be at peace with all men.***

In some ways, I was exhilarated, knowing that I really did have a father who loved God and would love me too. But on the other side, I wondered if he would reject me as I thought he had done in those early years. It took me until June, just before Father's Day, to work up the courage to send him a note. My Dad called on Father's Day, after receiving my posting. I was overwhelmed by his call and his acceptance of me, as well as with the joy of our new relationship. As only God could have arranged it, Dad was in charge of the Department of Agriculture's task force responsible for disposing of all of the excess grain as a result of the Russian grain embargo in 1980. His temporary assignment to the DC area, while we were stationed at Ft. Detrick, Maryland, was my opportunity to get to know my father as a Christian brother. It was amazing to see how God orchestrated and coordinated the details to facilitate the reunion and to bless me in my new relationship with my earthly father. We loved each other from the start and, when his wife was introduced into the mix, she was the wise 'mother' in Christ for whom I longed. Our meeting was more than I ever expected, and my husband and our daughters, five and three years old, warmed to our new family members as rapidly as I did. Jesus made a difference in our lives and in our relationships with one another. I was overwhelmed by what God had done in my father's life. This transformation was demonstrated by the fact that several years after their time in D.C., Dad retired from the Department of Agriculture, and he and his wife moved to Australia to serve five years as missionaries with the Navigators, an international and interdenominational Christian ministry.

The memory of this wonderful beginning continues to bless me as I see how God reconciled us to Himself first, and then, approximately seven years after my conversion, God orchestrated an event in history to bring Dad to Washington so that we could be reconciled to one another. Only God could have planned the entire incident from the Christmas card to the Father's Day card to the Russian grain embargo! That special time in DC marked a beginning of healing for me. I learned to forgive Dad, in the same way Christ had forgiven me, and I began to heal from all of the bitterness and rejection I had felt through the years.

Mother, however, was not as pleased with the reunion as I was. She was still bitter over the painful divorce and cautioned me to "wait and see" how my father would act toward me! I learned to reserve my comments regarding my father and stepmother when in my mother's presence, out of respect for her feelings.

Years went by and my relationship with my dad continued to thrive. In many ways, I felt closer to my father than to my mother. The love of Christ had truly united our hearts toward one another. In the meantime, the great divide was expanding in my relationship with Mother, as she pursued an opposite way of life.

My daughters, on the other hand, both of whom attended college in Mississippi, were able to develop deeper relationships with their grandmother by visiting her on weekends during the school year. Their visits were rich, full of laughter and sweet memories. In my view, this was a mixed blessing. Of course, I wanted my girls to know their grandmother better, but I was genuinely concerned that they would be wooed from the solid foundation of the Bible that they had learned while growing up in our home.

In 1998, our youngest daughter returned to northern Virginia after graduating from college, and fell in love with a young man she had met at a singles Bible study in Springfield, Virginia. After her engagement, the wedding was planned for July 6, 2002. Of course, all sets of grandparents were invited to the event, and thus began a new crisis, a real conflict!

I admit I made some critical mistakes in the way I handled the event. I really did not think my mother would even come to the wedding. She had not been able to attend any of our events in the past, and I assumed, bitterly, that she would not come to this event either. My stepfather was still alive and the two of them were elderly with the result that they had limited the majority of their travels for the past few years. I had no reason to suspect that my Mother would come to the wedding, except that she was the bride's maternal grandmother! I assumed that Mother's rejection of me and my faith would transfer to a rejection of her granddaughter during this faith-filled event as well. With those assumptions, I invited my dad and his wife to stay with us in our home. Later, I realized my mistake, but it was too late to undo it. Mother DID want to come! How surprised I was to hear the news, and then I became fearful of what emotions and drama the gathering would provoke!

The 'wedding-war' was unique! We watched the spiritual warfare unfold with every phone call to Mom. She would talk to my husband and say that I had said such and such. I would call back to make peace and she would say that my husband had indicated such and such. The calls went back and forth as Mother tried to stir up trouble in our family. It finally became evident that Mother was really baiting me to get so angry with her that I would tell her not to come to the wedding! At that point, I set my mouth NOT to say those words, regardless of the pressure, and I tried to maintain some peace in the relationship. It was not until later that I understood the reason for her behavior.

Mother had not seen, nor heard from my father since the divorce in 1953. Her wounded heart and anger toward my father were unresolved, and though years had intervened, she was still impacted by the marital scars of the past. Mother did not want to see my dad and felt that I was pushing her into the encounter by inviting both of them to the wedding. However, something must have made her realize that the die was cast because she made a 180 degree turn just weeks before the wedding and stunned us all! Mother actually called my father in California. She did not want the wedding to be about their relationship she said, so she wanted to talk to Dad, to break the ice, before they saw each other for the first time in over 50 years! By her act of reconciliation, Mom actually forgave him for the past, and, seeing them being kind and thoughtful toward one another at the wedding was a miracle that only God could have orchestrated. That was one of the noblest acts performed by my mother that I can recall. They got along together like two old chums. Incidentally, both parents had lost an eye: Dad from a childhood accident involving a stray rock, and Mother from her furniture reupholstering accident. The family enjoyed the preciousness of seeing the two of them trying to sit on the best side of each other in order to optimize each other's restricted vision. I stood in awe of God as I experienced the joy of my youngest daughter's covenant of marriage, and Mother and Dad's reconciliation. Two very special events that God had arranged just for us!

The relationship was further healed when in more recent years my dad began having symptoms of Alzheimer's disease. Once again, my mother made a difficult, but kind-hearted, call to my stepmother to offer help if it should be needed. God alone created the climate and the timing for these wonderful and extraordinary occurrences of forgiveness and healing. This manifestation of His great power prepared me for even greater works of His that were yet to come in my mother's life!

Mother and Tom's mother holding Beka, 1974

Dad and me, 1979

VI
THE CALL: THE MIRACLE BEGINS!

Just as each day brims with your beauty, my mouth brims with praise.
Psalm 71:8 (TM)

I must explore another important and relevant topic as I begin this next chapter. In order for the reader to understand my position, it is imperative that I explain the difference in seeking the guidance of a medium versus the guidance of the Holy Spirit. Jesus said when He was preparing the disciples for His crucifixion, "*I will ask the Father, and He will give you another Helper, that He may be with you forever; that is the Spirit of truth, whom the world cannot receive, because it does not see Him or know Him, but you know Him because He abides with you and will be in you*" (John 14:16–17). The word 'Helper' is translated from the Greek word *parakletos* and is also rendered as 'Counselor,' or one who gives support such as an adviser, strengthener, encourager or advocate. He is not an 'it,' but the third person of the Trinity along with the Father and Son. He is the Holy Spirit and is God, as "truly a Person distinct from the Father as the Son is."[32] Though there are many things we do not understand about the Spirit (and that are also outside the scope of this book), we do know His role in the life of a believer in Jesus Christ. J.I. Packer succinctly summarizes this role in his book, *Concise Theology*:

> Witnessing to Jesus Christ, glorifying him by showing his disciples who and what he is (John 16:7-15), and making them aware of what they are in him (Rom. 8:15-17; Gal. 4:6) is the Paraclete's central ministry.

[32] Packer, J. I. *Concise Theology: A Guide to Historic Christian Beliefs*. Wheaton, IL: Tyndale House, 1993.

> The Spirit enlightens us (Eph. 1:17-18), regenerates us (John 3:5-8), leads us into holiness (Rom. 8:14; Gal. 5:16-18), transforms us (2 Cor. 3:18; Gal. 5:22-23), gives us assurance (Rom. 8:16), and gifts us for ministry (1 Cor. 12:4-11). [33]

We also know that He will teach us (John 14:26), guide us into truth (John 16:13), and He will glorify Jesus, the Son (John 16:14). These are the very things a medium cannot, and will never be able to do.

A medium does not promote Jesus Christ, nor point toward a life of holiness. Sin itself, and even the concept of sin, is ignored, justified, or denied entirely. Mediums cannot deal with sin issues because they are actually allowing themselves to be used as the tools of the enemy, who is attempting to lead his victims away from God. The counterfeit guidance of the medium is superficial and involves seeking wisdom from a demonic source, rather than from God.

We can be easily deceived. C.S. Lewis notes "There are two equal and opposite errors into which our race can fall about the devils. One is to disbelieve in their existence. The other is to believe, and to feel an excessive and unhealthy interest in them. They themselves are equally pleased by both errors, and hail a materialist or magician with the same delight."[34] Finding our balance according to the Scriptures is vital. Satan works through the extremes of promoting either a complete denial of sin or a pushing toward perfection through works. The Holy Spirit convicts of sin, leads to the cross for confession, and the Father removes the guilt or punishment due the sinner as the result of His Son's blood shed on the cross for the forgiveness of sin (John 16:7-15, Heb. 9:22). Satan continues to beat up the victim with the transgressions, but the Spirit encourages an honest assessment of the sinful situation and ministers healing and strength to the one who turns from his sin.

---

[33] Packer, "God Revealed as Lord of Grace," "Paraclete"

[34] Lewis, C.S. *The Screwtape Letters.* HarperCollins Pub., NY. 2001. Preface, IX.

God knows what is best for us and wants to guide us in the decisions of our lives and He does it through His Word and His Holy Spirit. Mediums offer a fraudulent and deceptive guidance, but God, through His Holy Spirit, offers guidance based on His unconditional love for us. No one knows us to the extent God does. He knows our past, present, and future. He knows the thoughts of our hearts, our failings, our loves, and desires. He knows what is best for us. Why would we go anywhere else for help in our time of spiritual need? We are safe with Him and His wisdom does not fail, because it is based on His all-encompassing love for us.

God uses predominately four methods to direct and guide believers in Jesus Christ: His written Word from the text of the Bible, prayer, godly counsel from other believers, and circumstances. Often, God will incorporate several of these techniques to confirm His will. After I have prayed and laid an issue before God, I go to my daily Bible reading. One of the things I love best about God is that, as I read consistently through the Bible, I find that the exact verses I need for direction are often in the very text I am reading for that day. Without consciously looking for an answer, I read the Word, and before long, a verse or section of Scripture will provide the very direction I had been seeking. In addition, on many occasions, circumstances open up and even my husband, as my spiritual adviser and counselor, will be in agreement with the direction. I also discern direction through a heavier prayer burden or concern in that area as I sense that God is asking me to do something new. The Holy Spirit will use all four of these elements to provide guidance for His people. What God asks us to do is to trust Him to lead us and wait for Him to respond to us in His time.

Do I sometimes make mistakes in discerning His will? Absolutely! And God understands my confusion as I attempt to distinguish my own inner noises and the enemy's voice from His directions. Jeremiah must have struggled with telling the difference himself and, as a result, he offers us some encouragement.

> **Jeremiah 32:6-8** And Jeremiah said, "The word of the Lord came to me, saying, 'Behold, Hanamel the son

> of Shallum **your uncle is coming to you**, saying, "Buy for yourself my field which is at Anathoth, for you have the right of redemption to buy *it*."' **Then Hanamel my uncle's son came to me** in the court of the guard according to the word of the Lord and said to me, 'Buy my field, please, that is at Anathoth, which is in the land of Benjamin; for you have the right of possession and the redemption is yours; buy *it* for yourself.' **Then I knew that this was the word of the Lord.**

Jeremiah thought he heard the words from God, but until the circumstances occurred that confirmed the word, he was not sure. At that time, Jeremiah was under guard in the palace courtyard and unable to go out among the people, so God brought Hanamel, Jeremiah's cousin, to Jeremiah to accomplish His will.

I feel the same way regarding the impressions I experience. I do not seek an impression, but if I discern something from the Scripture that I think the Lord is speaking to my heart, I write it down in my journal, and wait. If God confirms it through circumstances, or in other ways apart from me manipulating the situation, then I know it is from the Lord. Remember, something from God is 100 percent correct. He does not fail in any detail. We can misunderstand or misinterpret, or want something so desperately that we can mistakenly perceive it as direction from the Lord. To protect ourselves from going astray, we do best to wait on the Lord to fulfill what we think is His direction in His timing, as Jeremiah did. If He doesn't confirm it, then it was not of Him.

We must also be on guard against false confirmations that come by following after our emotions or allowing our feelings to lead us as we make decisions, for these can often be misinterpreted by young believers who have not had *their senses trained to discern good and evil* (Heb. 5:14). The key is to discern what is in line with God's character and God's will. Our answers and directions will always agree with His ways. Proverbs has much to say about the heart and also regarding wise and foolish men. A wise man will learn not to *trust in his own heart* (one's inner self, inclination, feelings, or emotions[35]), as some psychologists would counsel, but rather to *walk wisely* (Prov. 28: 26). Proverbs 3:5-6 instructs us where to place our trust: *Trust in the Lord with all your heart and do not lean on your own understanding. In all your ways acknowledge Him, and He will make your paths straight.*

As the years passed, our lives took on new dimensions. By 2010, my husband and I were in-laws to two wonderful young men who loved and provided for our daughters, and we were grandparents of two delightful granddaughters, one per couple. We could not have been more pleased to see God working in the lives of our immediate family members, bringing the young ones to faith in Him and seeing their parents grow more in love with God and with each other.

In the midst of our busy lives, with both of us working full time, we had made time to visit with Mother two or three times each year. My husband's wonderful Christian mother had died in 2006, so much of our filial attention was focused on my mother. For several years, I traveled to Mississippi to celebrate Mother's Day with my mother, thus leaving the celebration of my own mothering to another time. The healing and forgiveness Mother had shown at my daughter's wedding, did not seem to fully embrace me and my faith. I found that meeting Mom in a neutral place, such as at my sister's home in Louisiana, made for a better visit with her. But I was disappointed that Mother did not seem to value these specially-timed visits, and she even appeared suspicious of my motives. Refusing to be pushed away, I then began to choose other times in my attempt to reach her.

Accepting for the time being that my relationship with Mom was not what I wanted it to be, I then began to focus on other unresolved issues in my life. One of these issues was the completion of my college degree, but not majoring in English as I had begun my college studies, but in Bible, which reflected my changed life. With my nest empty of children, my heart growing more full of my love for the Lord, and my desire to learn more

35 Strong, James. *A Concise Dictionary of the Words in the Greek Testament and The Hebrew Bible.* Bellingham, WA: Logos Bible Software, 2009. 3820.

about Him, His ways, and His Word through the Scriptures, I felt that the time was now ripe for me to finish my degree. After a year and one half of intense study, I graduated with a Bachelor of Science degree in Bible, Christian Life and Ministry, from Lancaster Bible College in Lancaster, PA, and gave thanks to God for giving me the strength, discipline, and time to complete such a task. I now have a better appreciation for my mother's struggle to obtain her degree so many years ago. Also, I began speaking at Christian Women's Clubs for Stonecroft Ministries in Virginia and throughout the central Atlantic coast area.

The Lord provided me with many speaking opportunities during this time. However, I received a very special, unique invitation in 2008. My husband's first cousin and her husband are members of a Baptist church in Jackson, Mississippi, where her husband serves as Minister of Music. I was thrilled to be invited to speak there and felt fortunate to have this unexpected time with my mother. I flew into the city just prior to five tornados hitting North Jackson. Mother picked me up at the airport, and although the weather looked ominous, we decided to stop by a nail salon to get a manicure while the storm passed over. The powerful wind swirled around us, and as I sat in the glassed-in shop, listening to the rattle of the back door of the small strip-mall establishment, I had such a marvelous sense of peace. I believed God had summoned me to Mississippi to speak at this event, and knew that I was indestructible until I had accomplished the mission.

The storm soon passed and we completed our trek home. Much to our surprise, a large portion of North Jackson had been devastated by the damaging winds. Uprooted trees and electrical lines were down all over, making the roads almost impassable, and homes were roofless with trees lying precariously across the now gaping holes in the roofs of once sturdy and welcoming homes. Devastation was all around. Mother and I dared not speak of what might await us a few blocks away at her house.

Mother's immediate neighborhood showed tremendous effects from the storm, but as we drew nearer to her house, we were surprised by the lack of damage to her own property. The home, art studio, and trees were totally unscathed! Not even a branch had fallen in my mother's yard! Damage was evident all around us, but Mother's yard was amazingly untouched by the winds and destruction. A miracle of no small impact!

I spoke at the women's retreat and stayed a week afterwards to visit with Mother. In the midst of helping neighbors and trying to keep our generator working because of a major power outage in her area, I never missed a moment to tell mother how fortunate she was. God alone had shown such mercy toward her. As it was, we had a marvelous time to visit without the distraction of TV or the frequent drop-in visits of her friends.

This background of both spiritual and physical struggle resulted in a real blessing as I persevered through the circumstances. It seemed to characterize my visits with my mother. Many times the spiritual battle was so great that I longed to escape the warfare, but a plane ticket that bound me to a certain departure date often was the only reason I stayed.

My trip to Mississippi in January 2010 began in much the same way. Mother had fallen in December of 2009, and had badly bruised her thigh and broken her upper arm. After her hospital stay, she had been released to a rehab center. Until that time, both of my sisters had been available to care for Mom, but I knew the time was coming for me to do my part. I knew that I did not want a knee-jerk reaction to an apparent need for Mother that my sisters were willing and capable of handling without my help. The old adage, *a need does not constitute a call,* heralded the caution I felt in my spirit. I knew that if God was not responsible for the call, it would be a clear disaster for me to race down to Mississippi to 'make all things right'! I waited on God to speak and watched him move in remarkable ways. To illustrate this, I offer my journal as a peek into God's amazing crescendo to the climax of yet another great miracle of the heart. Only God could have ordained such a marvelous event to show forth His glory!

I felt God urging me to stay home from church in Virginia this particular Sunday morning, and as I lingered longer in personal worship, praise, and prayer, I felt God speaking to me through my regular and consistent reading of His Word. I was specifically asking God to tell me when I should go to Jackson to help my sisters care for Mother. God used this Sunday morning to set me apart and prepare me for the coming adventure. My journal entry for that day was:

Journal Entry:
Sunday, January 24, 2010

Good morning, Lord. The Psalmist says You are great and greatly to be praised. You certainly are all I need for today and after You, I have no need. You are my God and my King, the Holy One, my Friend.

Thank You for calling me YOUR friend. You are amazing! How You could befriend someone so small and beneath You, is amazing. I would have avoided me…tossed my coin into the cup of a more promising beggar. But You chose me, knowing all You know about me. You have been beside me even when I failed to acknowledge You. Lord, please carry me all the way to the last breath and then let me enjoy Your presence forever. This is such a special time on earth that You have given to me. Please help me live what time I have left, proclaiming You in every place. Please show this small ant how to be one that honors You with every breath. Carry me on Your enormously strong back, Lord, as an elephant carries an ant.

Make me a fresh wineskin with which to pour in Your fullness, Your Spirit. I am an aging woman and I have lived over half my life. One would say it is too late for me to bring You honor and glory. My days are almost over in the scheme of life, yet Lord, I so desire to be a woman who honors You in every way. Please help me…show me how and remove the scales from my eyes. I love You and need You.

Lord, also - Mom is in the nursing home with water on her lungs and heart, declining in health. When do You want me to go down to help? What is Your desire? Please grant me/us wisdom to know when the time is right.

I love You, Lord. I will stay here and enjoy Your presence this morning... worshipping You through the music and reading Your Word. This is my church, my secret worship this morning. You truly are the greatest thing in all my life.

Lord, on Friday Cassie [our first granddaughter] *and her little friend Mia were with me. I was so tired and Tom* [my husband] *was sick at home...me too. Lord, I laid down, as Cassie napped before Mia's arrival, and asked for Your sweet touch, for Your strength and energy to give to the little girls. Lord, just like Cassie sometimes puts her face up to mine so that we are eye to eye almost, I felt You take Your hands and cup my face as we were eye to eye, cheek to cheek. Lord, I wept as You granted me the strength I needed for the afternoon. You are so good to me. You are my all in all and the first One I run to when my heart hurts or I am perplexed. You are the true Lover of my Soul and I am a fool when I choose something other than You as my first love. Lord, sitting in Your presence is so sweet, but what do I do with the go-ing part of the commission in this specific situation? Please send me at the right time. I look to You for the call. I know You will empower me as I keep my eyes on You and You will supply the words as I need them in each situation that You place me in... You are responsible for the outcome. I simply obey. I love You, Lord, for Your sweet assurances. I look to You for grace to move.*

Mark. 2:27-28 *Jesus said to them, "The Sabbath was made for man, and not man for the Sabbath. "So the Son of Man is Lord even of the Sabbath."*

"The Sabbath was made for man, not man for the Sabbath." You are funny to tell me directly. You are Lord of the Sabbath. I love You for Your direct answers. I am more in Your sweet presence here than I would be if I fussed to dress and race out to an hour of church - form and pretense - to look more spiritual to our kids. Forgive me for that one, Lord. I know that was a part of my motive this morning. But I so want You to know that I choose You first over all...even them. You alone are my God, not the opinions of my kids or even the family. You have given me such sweet time before You this morning. Though I do not want to forsake the

assembling of believers, I am mindful that my motives must be right before You...and that You even see those hidden things in my heart...things that get mixed up with my emotions. Thank You for revealing even that to me this a.m.

Today is our birthday celebration for Beka [our oldest daughter]. *She is 36 and beautiful...a loving mother and the wife of such a wonderful man. You picked him well for her! I love the way You pick for us when we are not mature enough to make a good choice for ourselves. You certainly did that for me. Thank You for Tom. I am so blessed by the life partner You gave me. You knew what I needed even when I didn't know my need. Who would have ever thought that You would do something so wonderful in our lives?? I am so grateful for the ways You have blessed us. . .*

I continued in prayer for my family as I read and interacted with the Scriptures.

Mark 3:5 *After looking around at them with anger, grieved at their* ***hardness of heart****, He said to the man, "Stretch out your hand." And he stretched it out, and his hand was restored.*

Lord, protect us all from ***hardness of heart****. Mark 3:5 tells me that it grieves You. Please soften and tenderize the hearts of our family from the smallest to the tallest - make us 100% in love with You, soft enough to receive from You and strong enough to resist the enemy. Forgive me for my hard heart that wants You to 'show me' Your great power and love. Lord, You ARE! What more needs to be said? You mean good for me. I do not need a display to know Your love. You are so beautiful and I am content to wait upon You for the timing that pleases You.*
I love You, Lord.
Your Stick - If you can use anything, Lord, You can use me. Use me as a simple stick or rod in Your hand to do Your will and give You glory.

Mark 3:13-14 *And He went up on the mountain and* ***summoned*** *those whom He Himself wanted, and they came to Him. And He* ***appointed*** *twelve, so that they would be with Him and that He could* ***send them out*** *to preach.*

Look at that, Lord! You chose and ***summoned*** *those You wanted to be with You so that You could* ***send them out to preach*** *. . . make that me too!*

The next day, I felt **summoned** by God as I began my trek to Mississippi to assist my mother in her recovery. My sister had called that very night I was seeking God's wisdom and indicated that she needed to return home. That was my call. My turn had arrived and I began to make flight reservations immediately. Mother's fall left her with a broken upper arm and a large internal hematoma on her leg. Suzie, the bulky and oversized English bulldog, who caused the accident, had broken Mother's fall, but Mom's injuries were serious enough for a brief hospital stay and weeks of rehabilitation at a rehabilitation and nursing home in Madison, Mississippi.

The care Mother was receiving began to concern us as we saw changes in her medication and large doses of pain medicine added to her regimen. Immediately after the injury, the pain medication was indicated, but Mother had previously received only small doses of drugs to ease her pain. Mother had a high tolerance for pain, as exemplified by her almost painless appendectomy the year before, and now she was drugged and swollen with bodily fluids. In addition, Mother had developed a deep 'manly' cough, as a young orderly later described her coughing spasms. Mother tended to develop congestive heart failure quickly, so it was important to keep her fluid reduction medication at a high dose, thus reducing the fluid and water retention that complicated her medical issues. That medication was cut in half by the rehab center doctor and Mother began to show signs of congestive heart failure.

God's Word in my devotional time continued to minister to my heart and to speak directly to my circumstances.

Journal Entry:
Monday, January 25, 2010

Looks like You ARE sending me out - I leave for Jackson at noon today. I need a haircut before leaving. I think I have everything. Please go before me. Buoy my heart and protect me from fear of the unknown. Help me be courageous. You are sending me. I trust You. Use me to really help Mom with her physical needs and to be a great blessing to her. Please protect me from contention and melt her hardness of heart. Help us get along and help me follow Your lead without trying to pass or run ahead of my Shepherd and Guide. Hold me, Lord. I am small, but Your hand is large enough for me. Cause Your Word to buoy me up on those late night drives home from the rehab center and Your love to be poured in me to love and minister in the details. Lord, my bag will be heavy. Please help me carry it.

My need is great, Lord. Help me rehearse Your goodness for I need to remember who You are in the midst of my need. You are my strength, my song, my agape love, my wisdom, my courage, my holiness, my protector, my companion, my provider, my path finder, my joy, my health, my all. You are the Bright and Morning Star. I love to wake to You! You are the Prince of Peace. I need Your perfect peace to accomplish this huge thing You have called me to do. You are the Mighty Warrior and You have defeated the enemy on my behalf. You are my Shepherd. Please guide me through these two weeks. You are my Defender; please shield and protect me from Mom's attacks and from Satan's attacks. You are my Great Physician. I trust You to keep me strong and healthy while working Your healing in Mom.

***Mark 3:11** Whenever the unclean spirits saw Him, they would fall down before Him and shout, "You are the Son of God!"*

Mark 3:11 - whenever unclean spirits saw You, they would submit to You. Please work the same with me as I enter in. Work another wonderful miracle like the one You worked my last trip home. I know You are more than able and I know You WILL help me. I have walked enough with You to know that I am not alone and that You will carry me. What more do I need? Cause me to go in power and strength and grant me favor as I accomplish the task You have called me to do. Hold my hand and help me through the tangles.

Mark 3:14-15 *And He appointed twelve, so that they would be with Him and that He could send them out to preach,* ***and to have authority to cast out the demons***.

Mark 3:14 and 15...INTERESTING...You called...summoned...Lord, You are fulfilling that verse specifically for me. Verse 15 says "and to have authority to cast out the demons." That's my mission, isn't it? You then appointed ordinary men...with ordinary personalities...like me. Thank You for this high privilege. You are doing this for me...for Mom. How You must love her!!

Mark 3:27 *But no one can enter the strong man's house and plunder his property unless he first binds the strong man, and then he will plunder his house.*

There is that authority again that You want me to take over Mom's house. Please lead me in this. I was thinking that Judy [my Christian sister-in-law who would pick me up at the airport] *and I could walk around the house binding the enemy and then 'plundering' his house in prayer. Thanks for the authority and I trust You with the rest. Please help me follow Your lead.*

Isaiah 29:24 *Those who err in mind will know the truth, and those who criticize will accept instruction.*

Isaiah 29:18 On that day the deaf will hear words of a book, and out of their gloom and darkness the eyes of the blind will see.

Lord, I am receiving these Scriptures as direct impressions from You. I don't know how you will use them, but I have written them down so I can document them.

Lord, make me a fisher of men...cause me to fish in deep waters where You direct...pull Mom/others from the sea of confusion and land her/them safely on eternity's shore. No, this work is not for sissies! Help me be brave, please.

I could not have even imagined how God would so specifically use His words to me from Isaiah within the next two weeks!! I was ready for what God would do, but had no idea how it would happen. I knew my own weaknesses, but I also knew the mighty power of God to override my weakness with His strength. I put my trust totally in Him and began to watch Him work His will through these unique circumstances.

As I wrote in my journal and interacted in prayer with the Scriptures, I in no way believed I was receiving a new revelation or was seeking a new interpretation for Scripture that had already been fulfilled by the nation of Israel or Christ Himself. Rather, I used the Scripture as a prayer prompt to direct my heart's desire. Ironically, much of what I recorded was what God actually accomplished in the midst of my circumstances. Looking back, I am encouraged to see how God ministered to me using His Word during this difficult time.

Many things happened during this time that challenged my understanding and did not fit neatly into my theological packaging. Some may question my conclusions regarding the 'strong man' in Mark 3:27. John Walvoord in his *Bible Knowledge Commentary* explains the parable from my perspective:

> The analogy in Mark 3:27 refuted [the scribes'] first accusation (v. 22) showing **in fact** (lit., "on the contrary") that the opposite was true. Satan is **the strong man.** His **house** is the realm of sin, sickness, demon possession, and death. **His possessions** are people who are enslaved by one or more of these things, and demons are his agents who carry out his diabolical activity. **No one can enter** his realm to **carry off** (*diarpasai,* "plunder") his possessions **unless he first** binds the strong man (shows he is more powerful). **Then he can rob** (*diarpasei,* "plunder") the realm, releasing the enslaved victims. At His temptation (cf. 1:12-13) and through His exorcisms Jesus demonstrated that He is the Stronger One, empowered by the Holy Spirit (cf. 3:29). His mission is to confront and overpower (not cooperate with) Satan and to deliver those en-

> slaved by him. [emphasis is in the text; not from this author][36]

Others may question my use of the word "authority" which was delegated to the disciples "to cast out the demons" (Mark 3:15). Steve Lemke, in his article in the *Holman Illustrated Bible Dictionary* states that:

> All authority could be characterized as either intrinsic or delegated. Intrinsic authority is dominion one exercises because it is innate in that person or inherent in the office held by that person. Because He is God and Creator of the universe, God has sovereignty and dominion over all things. Only the triune God has purely intrinsic authority. Delegated authority is given from one who has intrinsic authority to one serving in an office or carrying out a function. Delegated authority is not in itself innately or inherently authoritative; it is authority derived from one whose authority is intrinsic. All authority is properly God's. All other authority is derived from Him (Matt. 9:8; John 19:11; Rom. 13:1–3; Jude 25).[37]

Jack Hayford goes even further in his *Bible Handbook* explanation of the Greek word used for authority, *exousia*:

> *Strong's #1849*: One of four power words (*dunamis, exousia, ischus,* and *kratos*), *exousia* means the authority or right to act, ability, privilege, capacity, delegated authority. Jesus had the *exousia* to forgive sin, heal sicknesses, and cast out devils. *Exousia* is the right to use *dunamis,* "might." Jesus gave His followers *exousia* to preach, teach, heal, and deliver (v. 15), and that authority has never been rescinded (John 14:12).

[36] Walvoord, John F., Roy B. Zuck and Dallas Theological Seminary. *The Bible Knowledge Commentary: An Exposition of the Scriptures.* Wheaton, IL: Victor Books, 1985. Mk 3:23–27.

[37] Lemke, Steve W. "Authority, Divine Authority", *Holman Illustrated Bible Dictionary*, ed. Chad Brand, Charles Draper, Archie England, Steve Bond, E. Ray Clendenen and Trent C. Butler. Nashville, TN: Holman Bible Publishers, 2003. 145-46.

> Powerless ministries become powerful upon discovering the *exousia* power resident in the name of Jesus and the blood of Jesus. [38]

I will leave the argument to others to resolve. I took a literal view as I interpreted the Scripture through the lens of faith.

[38] Hayford, Jack W. and Thomas Nelson Publishers. *Hayford's Bible Handbook.* Nashville, TN; Atlanta, GA; London; Vancouver: Thomas Nelson Publishers, 1995. "Power."

VII
WEEK ONE: STRUGGLE

God, don't just watch from the sidelines. Come on! Run to my side!
Psalm 71:12 (TM)

The story continues to unfold in my journal:

Journal Entry:
Tuesday, January 26, 2010

Mom's house - Arrived yesterday. Entered the strong man's house and plundered his property by taking authority over the strong man in the name of Jesus Christ. Judy and I prayed as we walked through the house and asked God to sweep it clean. Then she took me out to Mom's rehab center via the highway, which I will be taking daily, rather than to confuse me with the back roads. Mom is better; looks good and strong; has a nasty cough with much mucus, but is doing pretty good. Arrived there around 5:30 p.m.-ish and got home at almost midnight, which was even later for me with the time zone change and my early rising. I was exhausted.

Tuesday did not flow as I expected it would. The morning after I arrived in Mississippi and, as I entered Mother's room for my first full day's visit/work, between deep and prolonged coughs, Mother informed me that she needed to see a doctor and wanted to go to the Emergency Room at St. Dominic Hospital in Jackson. Off we went, championed by the excellent physical therapy and day staff at the rehab center, and transported via ambulance to the Emergency Room at St. Dominic Hospital. I wondered what God had in store for us as a result of this shift in venue.

During this time of increased pain medication, Mother had developed a drug dependency. She would have deplored this addiction if she had been in her right mind, but anxiety, hopelessness, and despair increased as she approached the time for her next dose of the drug. This state of apprehension made being with her excruciating for approximately forty-five minutes to an hour before her timed medication, and if the meds were late in being administered, her anxiety intensified. I had never experienced the effects of drug addiction and tried to reason with my mother. Of course, individuals addicted to drugs can't be reasoned with and this proved to be true with mother too. I slowly began to understand more of the difficulties involved in this new challenge. My assigned responsibility by the family was to be certain that the diuretic was not decreased, nor the pain medication increased. Actually, our desire was that the pain medication be decreased. I then knew that my job was not going to be easy, nor was it within the normal parameters of a regular hospital stay.

Emergency Room X-Rays determined that Mother had pneumonia in one lung and fluid in her other lung. She was to be admitted to the hospital, but as the hours ticked by waiting for admission and a room, Mother began to exhibit symptoms of the addiction. Her hunger for the drug was not satisfied right away, so she decided to get dressed and just get out of there! Finally, a dose came and she was placated until we moved to her room on the fourth floor. The wonderful nursing staff at this new location in the hospital made up for the long delay in the ER. Linda was our wonder-nurse who helped us settle into what would be our new abode for the next ten days. Linda's compassion exceeded anything I had ever seen as she crushed the large tablets that were difficult to swallow and fed Mother her meds mixed with ice cream. I spent the night at the hospital on a couch, as Mom coughed and struggled all night trying to get comfortable. Neither of us was able to sleep.

On Wednesday, the family made an official request for Mother's pulmonary doctor to consult with the assigned doctor from the rehab center. The doctor came in to see Mother in the afternoon and as Mother told him about her injury and rehab experience, his eyes brightened! He said, "You just gave me the important clue!" and then quickly examined her Vienna sausage-like toes. Within the hour, Mother was sent to have a CT scan of her chest and an ultrasound of her legs. Mother was diagnosed with small blood clots in her legs from the internal hematoma, which caused the immense swelling in her legs, and also with a blood clot in her lung, along with the pneumonia and the excess fluid. Her medications were changed immediately to reflect the new diagnosis, and from that point, Mother began to heal.

Mother also became annoyed with me, thinking that I was standing between her and her much desired medications...especially the pain pills. In addition, she thought that I was insisting that she be released quickly. Actually, my concern was that we move her out of the rehab center by Friday, before we were charged for additional days while she was in the hospital. We were both exhausted from lack of sleep, as evidenced by our shortness of patience with one another, so I went home to get a good sleep for the first time since our arrival at the hospital.

Journal Entry:
Thursday, January 28, 2010

Good morning, Lord. I am still tired, but awake. It is hard with the time change to catch everyone on the phone and still rest. I talked and prayed with Tom this morning before he left for work.

Lord, I seem incapable of getting myself together. I don't want to go into it, but Mom and I are at odds. I came home to rest last night, instead of staying all night. We both needed the rest. Lord, I feel like this is warfare. Please help me rise up to deal with it. I need You, Lord.

Thank You for Tom and for helping me to love and forgive Mom. Lord, I look to You for help...no one or nowhere else. Please encourage me with Your love...with Your Word. Listening to the Scripture music is just what I need. How You have blessed me! Thank You, Lord.

Thank You for helping me humble my heart and for the prayer I had concerning Mom this a.m. Help me continue to serve her in love. When I woke, I felt so hard hearted. Thanks for taking this mean and selfish woman - ME - to the cross for healing again. You alone are my God. Who could put up with me like You do?

Lord, if You can feed 5000 on just a few scraps of food, feeding me emotionally and spiritually is nothing. You have nourished me this morning by Your Word and Your people. Thank You for the beauty of a walk with You. You keep me on my face before You. Now, please take the scraps of myself that I offer You and break me...use me to feed others with my words and my actions today. I offer my all, though small, and ask for Your great work to be accomplished in me today. Help me know my boundaries and walk in love.

Please protect me from my own hard heart. I have seen You do so much. I know You are God. Please cause me to be quick to humble myself at the proper time. Don›t allow me to build walls between You and me. Break me and keep me broken. Let me hold on to the fringe this day...cause me to walk in Your footsteps. I love You, Lord.

I talked with my youngest sister, regarding Mother's attitude toward me. When I arrived at the hospital that morning, my sister called and began to refresh Mother's mind as to the state of affairs...the medication changes and addiction issues. Mother was more alert and repeated "I didn't know that" or "I forgot that." Our relationship improved a bit as a result, and she began to see me more as her advocate, rather than her antagonist.

With Mother beginning to heal and the medications improving her well-being, I was able to escape for a few hours to feed and refresh her African Gray birds and also to move her things out of the rehab center. The family had determined that when Mother was released from the hospital, we would simply take her home. She had already completed the majority of the physical therapy regimen and would have home-care therapy when she was released. I took a few hours off to run errands and to complete the removal of Mother's things from the center, and then returned to sit by her bed and meet her needs. A constant stream of friends came through to visit Mother during this time. How grateful we were for the kindness they showed to us. Many of these friends were regular visitors and attendees of a class Mother taught on *The Course in Miracles.* My sister-in-law and my husband's first cousin were also sweet refreshment for mother and me. In addition, the aides, nurses, and respiratory technicians provided wonderful diversion from the monotony of the day. Still Mother's terrible cough, although better, was continually present.

Journal Entry:
Friday, January 29, 2010

Lord, yesterday was a great day for Mom...certainly, she is getting better. Thank You for that. I am going to move quickly to get to the hospital this morning before the meds come. Thank You for what You are doing. Please keep the doctor away until I get there and delay the meds until I can be there to see what they are giving her. Thank You, Lord.

Isaiah 31:9 "His rock will pass away *because of panic, And his princes will be terrified at the standard," declares the Lord, whose fire is in Zion and whose furnace is in Jerusalem.*

You are the Rock in whom I put my trust. Isaiah 31:9 says that "his rock will pass away because of panic." You are my Rock that stands between me and the hard place. You are holy and You are my help. I put my trust in the strength of my life - YOU! Please cause Mom's eyes to see You, her ears to hear Your voice, and her 'rock,' her confidence, to pass away. Prevent the evil one from controlling her and grant her true peace. Please help her see truth. I rely on You, Lord. I am totally dependent on You. You are so good.

While Isaiah 31:9 actually refers to the defeat of the Assyrian army, I used the words to pray back what was on my heart.

Journal Entry:
Saturday, January 30, 2010

Good morning, Lord. I am so glad to be resting better...8 full hours this morning! Amazing for me, since I am normally on a 7 hour regimen at home. Lord, I so miss my family this morning...I miss their arms and their love. I know You must have been homesick too. Please hold my heart. I have another week to get through. I am happy to serve, but I am homesick. I long to be home with Tom and the kids. How blessed I am to have such a loving family. This is the painful part.

Lord, thank You for Mom's recovery. She is getting so much better and the drug dependency issue has diminished. . . Lord, please invade her thinking and show her that she is trusting in chariots and horses, rather than the King of Kings! I do not know what is going on, but I know that there are fish in the lake without seeing them jump. And I know that You are answering prayer without me seeing it happen on the surface. You have answered so much prayer already. I trust You for the full picture. Please reveal Yourself in her picture. Connect the dots and show her without me telling her. Surround her with bold Christians who will speak truth in love. Lord, only You can answer this great prayer. I love You so much.

Once again, I lift my cup to You. Please fill it for I am so empty today. Cause my eyes to only see You and to look to none other to fill my cup. Grant me favor and joy in this service and please help me be the big girl in every aspect. Make me brave and courageous and use this to prepare me to speak to the group in February. Lord, I feel so inadequate. Please raise me up and prepare me to enter this opportunity with confidence in YOU and joy in the doing.... I will wait upon You. (I had a speaking engagement in February, and my departure from Mississippi was timed to make that event.)

Thank You for Tom and the girls. Bless our ladies, large and small, and the boys. Grow our family to love You more and help us all to live Your Word more and to cherish You with all of our hearts. Renew our passion for You and make us bold proclaimers of the riches of Your grace. How we need You to transform us all into a clear reflection of You. Be our joy today. Hold each of us and renew the flame of our love. Lord, I long for their embrace. Please let me feel Yours and be filled and satisfied today. Holy is Your name! And You will not forget Your beloved in this place of need.

Forgive me for any pride or self-righteousness. Help me walk humbly. I have none but You to rely upon and, Lord, I am leaning heavily upon You...carry me, Lord.

Isaiah 32:1-6 *Behold, a king will reign righteously And princes will rule justly. Each will be like a refuge from the wind And a shelter from the storm, Like streams of water in a dry country, Like the shade of a huge rock in a parched land.* ***Then the eyes of those who see will not be blinded, And the ears of those who hear will listen. The mind of the hasty will discern the truth, And the tongue of the stammerers will hasten to speak clearly. No longer will the fool be called noble, Or the rogue be spoken of as generous. For a fool speaks nonsense, And his heart inclines toward wickedness: To practice ungodliness and to speak error against the Lord, To keep the hungry person unsatisfied And to withhold drink from the thirsty.***

Isaiah 32:1-6 - Lord, these seem to be words for me to pray back. You will rise up and grant sight to the spiritually blind and hearing to the spiritually deaf. You will bring her to the place of listening and she will discern truth. You will turn the table so that the 'fool' will no longer be called noble. Lord, Mom is the foolish one to put her hope in what does not satisfy and to teach others to drink from emptiness. Only You can reveal that. I bow before You and wait for the fish to jump. I love You, Lord. Please grant me hope.

Mark 8:22-25 *And they came to Bethsaida. And they brought a blind man to Jesus and implored Him to touch him. Taking the blind man by the hand, He brought him out of the village; and after spitting on his eyes and laying His hands on him, He asked him, "Do you see anything?" And he looked up and said, "I see men, for I see them like trees, walking around." Then again He laid His hands on his eyes; and he looked intently and was restored, and began to see everything clearly.*

Mark 8:22-25 - Please spit on my mom's eyes and lay Your holy hands on her eyes. Use Your holy power to create eyes that see and open what has been closed for so long. Soften what has been hardened and create a love for You that only You can manufacture.

Mark 8:33 *But turning around and seeing His disciples, He rebuked Peter and said, "Get behind Me, Satan; for you are not setting your mind on God's interests, but man's."*

Mark 8:33 is for me as well....help me set my mind on Your interests, rather than man's (or MY) interests.

Saturday was an unremarkable day with friends and family dropping by at odd times. These delightful people helped our day go by smoothly. I was still waiting for the fulfillment of those marvelous words from God's Word!

Journal Entry:
Sunday, January 31, 2010

Jackson, Mississippi - Mom is still in the hospital. I am wondering about the meds. The weekend staff appear to be callous and uncompassionate. Lord, please be Mom's advocate. Please help her and tell me what to say or how to pursue helping her. I hope to dress and get in this morning.... maybe go home in the afternoon to feed the birds. Lord, please lead me in this. I need Your help.

Later: 12:30 p.m. - home and in bed. Mom told me to go home. It hurt, but I think she wanted me to go so she could get her pain meds. I confronted her by saying that her comment was rude. She began back peddling and saying how much she loved me...something I didn't believe at all at that time. She also pleaded on the phone with Mary [the older of my two younger sisters] *to come up tomorrow...again showing her lack of joy at having me around. Lord, I want to honor her, but loving and liking her are two different things. Help me love and honor her, regardless of how I feel. Forgive me for my bitter attitude right now. Please help me rest and then go back with renewed zest and joy.*

Mother told me to go home at approximately 10 a.m., which I did immediately. I went back to the hospital at 4:30 p.m. Friends were present when I returned, although Mother was still grumpy and insulted me in front of them. The day was emotionally exhausting and I was eager to go home at 8:45 p.m. I was irritated at the way she had treated me all day, and Mom knew I was unhappy with her. I had established a pattern as I left the hospital each evening of praying for Mom before walking out of the door. The day had been so hard that I thought I would just slip out of the room without prayer. As I was leaving this time, Mother asked me if I was going to pray for her. Honestly, I did not want to pray. My heart was hurting, but I knew the Holy Spirit was speaking to me through her request. I silently humbled my heart, confessed my hurt and pride, and quickly asked the Holy Spirit for words. I prayed for her that evening and continued to pray for her each time before I left her. Sometimes my heart was breaking with her rude treatment, but I chose to obey God rather than listen to my emotions, to set my mind on God's business, not my own self-centered concerns.

VIII
THE MIRACLE WEEK

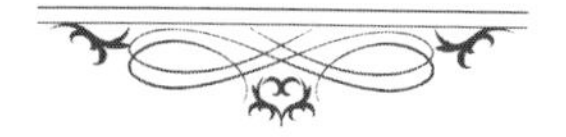

I'll write the book on your righteousness,
talk up your salvation the livelong day,
never run out of good things to write or say.
Psalm 71:16 (TM)

Journal Entry:
Monday, February 1, 2010

Good morning, Lord. Each day here brings a new development. Yesterday ended better.

Talked to Deb [my youngest sister]. *She has a way of putting it all together for me. I realized after my discussion that Mom is just as difficult for all of us. Anyway, I took her advice and called Mom first before going back. Had dinner at a nice deli, my first real meal since arriving...then headed back to the hospital.*

Lord, my heart is so heavy. My eyes are mega swollen...maybe allergy, who knows. Please touch my eyes, Lord, and make them better. Remove the swelling and help me move today. Touch me again and renew my love for I have none for today. I come to You empty, asking for Your filling. Please energize me and move me through this day. [As I was cleaning Mom's birdcages, a gust of wind from an open door had blown the droppings up into the air...and into my eyes. I was not immediately aware that the irritation in my eyes was due to this incident.]

I prayed with Tom this morning. Mom may come home today...but most probably on Tuesday or Wednesday. Lord, please call the time. Only You can cause all of this to work together. BE my great joy today. Feed my heart with good things from Your Word. I look to You for help.

Mark 10:43-45 *"But it is not this way among you, but whoever wishes to become great among you shall be your servant; and whoever wishes to be first among you shall be slave of all. For even the Son of Man did not come to be served, but to serve, and to give His life a ransom for many."*

Mark 10:43-45 - You said that whoever wishes to be great must be a servant. Lord, I am a lousy servant. Please help me die to self and live to You.

Mark 10:51 *And answering him, Jesus said, "What do you want Me to do for you?" And the blind man said to Him, "Rabboni, I want to regain my sight!"*

Mark 10:51 - a blind beggar. Grant my mom sight; do the impossible and grant me hope and trust in You alone as I wait upon You.

Mark 10:27 *Looking at them, Jesus said, "With people it is impossible, but not with God; for* ***all things are possible with God."***

Isaiah 34:11 *But pelican and hedgehog will possess it, and owl and raven will dwell in it; and He will stretch over it the* ***line of desolation and the plumb line of emptiness.***

Isaiah 34:11 - The line of desolation and the plumb line of emptiness - Lord, please remove the line of desolation from this household and the plumb line of emptiness...reveal the great need to Mom and supply as only You can do.

Isaiah 35:3 *- Encourage the exhausted [that would be me] and strengthen the feeble [me again]. Say to those with anxious heart, take courage, fear not. Behold your God will come....*

Thank You for Your encouragement!

Isaiah 35:5 *Then the eyes of the blind will be opened and the ears of the deaf will be unstopped.*

Isaiah 35:5 – CAUSE the eyes of the blind to be opened and the ears of the deaf to be unstopped in this house!

Lord, I am running out of steam - physical, emotional, and spiritual steam.

I continued to pull words from the Scriptures and to pray them back to the Lord. Of course, the true context of these verses would be different than the way in which I applied them to my mother and me.

Later in the evening: *Lord, this was an exceptional day. I am reading the book that Judy lent me [Same Kind Of Different As Me[39]] to Mother! It is a good story and is something Mother can identify with. Amazing that this could be something that draws us closer together! Thank You for what You are doing. My eyes were so swollen today...painful, but it was an opportunity to lay down my vanity. Thank You, Precious Lord, for helping me to keep moving. You supplied in a wonderful way. You are actually working a miracle. Thank You for allowing me to have a part in it. I love You, Lord.*

Lord, my eyes are still a problem. Please work Your healing even overnight. I commit myself to You.

I had taken a book to the hospital, *Same Kind Of Different As Me,* by Denver Moore and Ron Hall, to return to Judy when she dropped by for a visit. It was a book I had borrowed, but could not get into and wanted to simply return it unread. During the long day at the hospital, I picked it up to read aloud to Mom. I thought I would read a bit and that she would lose interest. Mom had not been interested when I had offered other CDs or DVDs during her hospital stay, so I had little hope that this would be any different. Her attention span was too short to listen for a sustained period of time. I really thought Judy would take the book

[39] Moore, Denver and Ron Hall. *Same Kind Of Different As Me.* Thomas Nelson: Nashville, 2006.

home with her when she dropped by for her visit. I could not have known how well Mother would receive the paperback book. She was riveted from the start.

Same Kind Of Different As Me is the true story of the relationship of a wealthy international art dealer, Ron Hall, and a homeless black man, Denver Moore. The telling of the story switches back and forth between the two men. At the insistence of his wife, Ron Hall becomes a volunteer at a homeless shelter and meets Denver there. They begin a friendship that grows into love and respect, and as they begin to tell their life stories, the relationship expands even more. The men, though worlds apart in their life-experiences, endure a tragedy together and teach each other lessons about life and faith. In the course of the book, Denver relates the horror stories of life as a sharecropper in the South during his childhood. The painful experiences and horrific images of that time influenced his direction in life and eventually led to his homelessness. Denver has a hard and impenetrable spirit, but through the loving persistence of Ron and his wife, Denver begins to soften toward people and then toward Christ.

This was a plot with which Mother could identify. She too had seen the inhumane treatment of Blacks in the South and was appalled at how such behavior was justified by the people and overlooked by the authorities. We would read a bit, stop and cry, tell our own experiences and then read some more. I was amazed at how positively Mother responded to this book.

Journal Entry:
Tuesday, February 2, 2010

Mary is coming up today. I look forward to seeing her. She will stay a few days to visit with me and then head home on Friday. Thank You for that kind company. Please bind us together and help us be loving and kind to Mom....especially help us battle in the heavenlies on Mom's behalf. Grow me here. Teach me Your ways...MAKE me a servant. I look to You alone for my help.

My eyes are still swollen...washed them out this a.m. and took an aspirin to help relieve the inflammation. Only You can heal my eyes. If You would have me go to a doctor, please open the door. I need You to lead. I am alone here and don't know where to go or what I need to do.

I think I will take my time this a.m. and get out for a walk before heading out to the store. Thanks for Mom - her life and her love for me/us. Thank You for the influence she has been for good to us. She taught me valuable principles to live by and I appreciate her investment in my/our lives. You planned my life and planted me in this home. You gave me a worthy gift with that placement and You have given me a worthy goal of loving my mom into the kingdom. Lord, I look to You for I can do nothing without You. You alone can make me loving and kind, Christlike, for I do not possess that in my own nature. Look with compassion on my mom and use me and Mary to be Your hands and feet to serve her. Show us how to be a powerhouse in this home to wrestle our mother from the grip of the enemy. Open our eyes. Don't let me be a fanatic, but a mature believer in You.

Isaiah 37:15-20 *Hezekiah prayed to the Lord saying,* ***"O Lord of hosts, the God of Israel, who is enthroned above the cherubim, You are the God, You alone, of all the kingdoms of the earth. You have made heaven and earth. Incline Your ear, O Lord, and hear; open Your eyes, O Lord, and see; and listen to all the words*** *of Sennacherib, who sent them to reproach the living God . . . Now, O Lord our God, deliver us from his hand that* ***all the kingdoms of the earth may know that You alone, Lord, are God."***

Isaiah 37:15-20 - prayed back on behalf of Mom...

Isaiah 37:26 *"Have you not heard? Long ago I did it, from ancient times I planned it. Now I have brought it to pass, that you should turn fortified cities into ruinous heaps."*

Isaiah. 37:26 - Lord, I am holding on to the fact that You have a plan in this and that You will not allow my mom to perish, but have everlasting life. Please cause Your zeal to accomplish this impossible task.

Mark 11: 22-26 *And Jesus answered saying to them, "Have faith in God. Truly I say to you, whoever says to this mountain, 'Be taken up and cast into the sea,' and does not doubt in his heart, but believes that what he says is going to happen, it will be granted him. Therefore I say to you, all things for which you pray and ask, believe that you have received them, and they will be granted you. Whenever you stand praying, forgive, if you have anything against anyone, so that your Father who is in heaven will also forgive you your transgressions. [But if you do not forgive, neither will your Father who is in heaven forgive your transgressions."]*

Mark 11:22-26 - Look, Lord!! The mountain and faith verses...My faith is in You, not my words, but in confidence that I have been heard and that You will act on my behalf. Lord, I believe. I know You are doing something with this mountain - uprooting the lies and deception and casting it into the sea. The mountain of unbelief in this house is being destroyed. The strong man is bound and his property has been plundered. Thank You, Jesus! "All things for which you pray and ask, believe that you have received them and they will be granted you." You go on to talk about forgiveness...Lord, I forgive my mom for the mistakes she made with me...mistakes I have been bitter about through the years. Forgive me, Lord, for brooding about things like that. I know You worked the placement...cause me to walk in love so that I too can get my sins forgiven.

Mary arrived and we began to pray together, both in the morning before going to the hospital, and in the evening after returning from the hospital. We also continued to pray with Mother before leaving her at the hospital each night. We were joined in prayer at the end of the day by a respiratory technician who was in the room administering Mom's treatment just before we left the hospital. When my sister and I needed to leave, we simply asked whoever was in the room if they would like to pray with us before we left. Several therapists were eager to be a part of our prayer for Mother. Mother was delighted to include them, and several times they too added their own prayers to ours. At that time, Mother did not verbally participate in our prayers, but would occasionally remind us of how, and where, she specifically needed God's helping hand.

Journal Entry:
Wednesday, February 3, 2010

Lord, how wonderful You are!! You are doing a wonderful work. Thank You for letting us be a part of it. Mom is still listening intently to the book. Please open her eyes as she listens. Cause questions to arise and, Lord, please help us answer her.

Mary arrived yesterday afternoon. We stayed at the hospital until 8:30 or so. Prayed with Mom before leaving...even her respiratory tech, Kajaun, joined us. Pretty cool. It is so obvious that You are doing a great work. Please do not let me rush it. I love You, Lord. I am amazed that You are answering so gently and lovingly. Please keep my heart humble and don't allow me to manipulate circumstances in any way.

Lord, last night I was so tired that I could not even think. Please help me stay alert and attentive. Please anoint me/us with Your Spirit and work a mighty work in us, as well as Mom....and let it flow to those who follow her. Cause a great revival in this area. Work the miracles of the heart here and don't forget Deb in the process. I so love You, Lord. Please reveal Yourself and help me wait upon You for the Big Reveal. Please feed me/us with Your Word as we move throughout the day. Let all be done to bring You glory...not for my/our glory. Forgive me for even thinking of my own glory. You alone deserve it! Please keep me bowed before You. Lord, I am empty and small. Please fill me with Your Spirit. Grant me an anointed tongue and cause me to speak truth in love. Amplify my small to work Your wonders. Let this ant ride on the back of the elephant...the strong and mighty God of the universe.

The Big Reveal came at last! God arranged a magnificent event for us to witness! The amazing day came on that Wednesday as we witnessed God's extraordinary work. Mother's heart had been softened by reading the book and God paraded His people one by one before her to pray for her and to point her to Christ. The most amazing part was when I asked a newly assigned technician what drew her to become a respiratory technician. Her story began with how she had been in a destructive relationship, and after a disastrous break-up, she had returned home, depressed and hopeless. Her mother encouraged her to apply for a job at a local restaurant, which was owned and operated by a devout Christian couple, in her small Mississippi hometown. The owners eventually led her to belief in Jesus Christ, and nurtured her for several years before she decided to become a respiratory technician. As Lindsay shared her story, silent tears ran down my cheeks. The presence of the Lord was so evident. Mother was captivated by Lindsay's words and asked question after question about her experience. Later, Lindsay told me she had not been assigned to floor duty in a long time. That morning, she was initially annoyed by the change in assignment, but after the conversation with my mother, she realized that it was indeed a God assignment. I could not tell Lindsay how her altered schedule had brought her to the bedside of one of the city's renowned spiritists, but I marveled at God's perfect timing for Mother!

After Lindsay left, Mary and I spoke openly with Mom regarding the sacrificial work of Christ on her behalf. She listened and asked questions and from that moment on, Mother's countenance changed, her treatment of me, and her openness to prayer and conversation about Christ changed totally. Mother's simple acknowledgement of her trust in Christ started her on a new path. Mom had been ***snatched from the jaws of the lion***! My sister and I were able to speak openly of redemption and when we prayed with Mother, she was in agreement with us and actively participated in thanking God for His goodness and in laying her petitions before Him. Mother trusted in her heart and confessed Jesus as Lord with her mouth in that hospital, and the Bible says that this confession "results in salvation." Ephesians 2:8 says that salvation is a gift of God and that we are saved through faith, not as a result of our own works.

Was all of this just wishful thinking or did God perform the miracle of new birth at that moment? Just like me, Mom had a long way to go to simply understand the biblical concepts, but she had begun the journey by accepting God's free gift of eternal life. When does God open the gates of heaven for a new believer? After we get cleaned up or when we simply confess Him with our mouths and put our trust in Him? A vivid illustration used by a former pastor demonstrates how we come to God with all of our baggage of sinful habits, false perceptions, and wounds from our pasts. The heavy load is not shed at the moment of salvation, but is eliminated when each issue is confronted in our lives and our minds are renewed by the washing of the word of God. I firmly believe that God orchestrated the entire event for our mother, and did it in the presence of my sister and me so that we would have the joy of seeing our mother trust in Him. We had fervently prayed through the years for her, and we stood in amazement as we watched God display His glory through answered prayers. My journal provides the wonder of that moment for us.

Journal Entry:
Thursday, February 4, 2010

Dearest Lord....sounds like rain out there!! Your spirit is raining down on us!! You are so good to me/us. I can hardly believe that You have so softened my Mom. Lord, You brought a young girl, Lindsay, by Mom's hospital room yesterday who boldly told us how she came to know You, and later Mom even asked Lindsay to pray for her. You did that!! Only You could have done such a wonderful thing! A Catholic priest and also a layman came by separately and prayed with Mom too. It was amazing to see Your line-up for Mom. Plus, the book we are reading is so good and it is saying all that we would ever have wanted to say regarding salvation. In addition, we, Mary and I, both had a chance to talk with Mom about sin, breaking Your law, and Your substitutional death. I have never been able to talk so freely to Mom. . . . Lord, Mom is "owning" her relationship with You, confessing You as her Lord and God. She is absolutely radiant in her red robe and joyful heart. I stand in awe of You!

Yes, Lord, I know I dabbled in a New Age program promoting psychic development for a while before I realized that Christianity and New Age thought were incompatible. You brought me out of that to the place of repenting of my sin and of renouncing the lies and deception, but what about Mom? Lord, please open her eyes and cause the blind to see. Only You can put this together and You appear to be doing just that! So keep me out of the way. Just bring someone else to say what she needs to hear. Someone she can receive from. You are so good to Mom. Your love for her is so great that You have allowed so many variables to speak to her already.

Mark 13:11 *"When they arrest you and hand you over, do not worry beforehand about what you are to say, but* ***say whatever is given you in that hour; for it is not you who speak, but it is the Holy Spirit."***

Isaiah 37:35 *"For I will defend this city to save it for My own sake and for My servant David's sake."*

Isaiah. 37:35 *Lord, You say You will defend this city to save it for Your own sake and for Your servant's sake....Lord, for Your own sake and my sake, maybe, would You please defend this property to keep deception and lies far from Mom? Please protect her here and allow Your Word to continue to grow in her heart. Please protect her.*

A few lines from the book we were reading appeared to speak directly to our situation with Mom. Denver, when asked what he thought of the first spiritual retreat he had ever attended, said, "I had to get away from where the devils lived before I could hear from God." So true for Mom!! There were other things in the book that appeared to be specifically appropriate to our experience, but there were two chapters at the end of the book that I thought would confuse Mother. As the skilled editor of the books I read to my children, I simply skipped paragraphs and pages that were meaningful to the authors, but would muddy the picture for my mother.

Journal Entry:
Friday, February 5, 2010

Good morning, Lord. Mom comes home today. We are trying to clean up and prepare for her homecoming. Lord, I fear we will lose ground gained when she returns, but You are able to defend her from the evil one and to continue to encamp around her. You are able to do for her what we are unable to even ask, so Lord, we commit her into Your hands. Please cause her to forsake her folly and to cling to the truth...the pursuit of the truth....You!! Lord, become her all in these last days. Only You can do this for her. Please raise up prayer warriors on her behalf and draw her into Christian fellowship. Cause her to seek YOUR face and not the face of her own will and rebellion.

Isaiah 40: 1-2 *"Comfort, O comfort My people," says your God. "Speak kindly to Jerusalem; And call out to her, that her warfare has ended, That her iniquity has been removed, That she has received of the Lord's hand Double for all her sins."*

*Isaiah 40:1-2 Are these Your words for us?? ....Comfort, O Comfort My people....speak kindly to Jerusalem.....**her warfare is ended; her iniquity has been removed**.*

Isaiah 40:10-11 *Behold, the Lord God will come with might, With His arm ruling for Him. Behold, His reward is with Him And His recompense before Him. Like a shepherd He will tend His flock, **In His arm He will gather the lambs And carry them in His bosom**; He will gently lead the nursing ewes.*

Isaiah 41:10 *Do not fear, for I am with you; Do not anxiously look about you, for I am your God. I will strengthen you, surely I will help you, Surely I will uphold you with My righteous right hand.'*

Isaiah. 41:10 - How lovely You are. You are my comfort and strength. Thank You for what You have done on our behalf.

Isaiah 42:9, 16 *"Behold, the former things have come to pass, Now I declare new things; Before they spring forth I proclaim them to you."* . . . ***I will lead the blind by a way they do not know, in paths they do not know I will guide them. I will make darkness into light before them and rugged places into plains. These are the things I will do, and I will not leave them undone.***

Mother was discharged from the hospital on Friday. Rob, my brother from Knoxville, Tennessee, and Jeff, Mary's husband, arrived to spend the weekend with Mother, my sister, and me. It was a delightful time together. I slept in the big king-sized bed with Mom and we continued to pray together each night. What a sweet and holy time! We also continued to read the final chapters in our book. Rob, Jeff, and Mary left Sunday morning, and Mother and I completed the book that afternoon.

Journal Entry:
Monday, February 8, 2010

Lord, I am going home today. I am amazed at what YOU have accomplished. You alone have done such marvelous deeds! I love and praise You!

Judy is picking me up to take me to the airport at 10:30 and I have much to do to prepare. Please help me accomplish much around the house to leave Mom in a good situation. I love You, Lord. I have had the most marvelous time with my Mom. We have prayed and talked, laughed and cried together. Thank You for the wonderful memories, and for the changes in our relationship. ONLY YOU!! More important than a relationship with me is that she has a relationship with You. Thank You, Lord. Time is running out and she appears to be more receptive than ever. Glory to YOU!!

Reading to Mother in the hospital, 2010

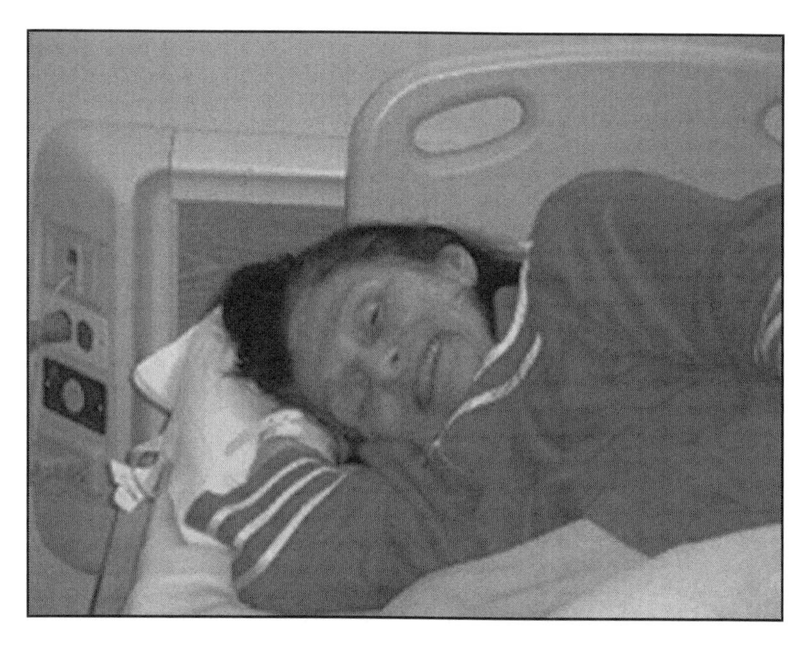

After Glow of Mom's Confession of Faith

IX
HOME

God, don't walk off and leave me
until I get out the news of Your strong right arm to this world,
news of your power to the world yet to come.
Psalm 71:18 (TM)

I left on a flight that flew into one of Washington DC's worst snow storms in history. My flight was scheduled during a small window of time between storms on February 8, and I returned without any delays or difficulty. The tickets were bought on January 24, 2010, before even the first cold wave hit the DC area, when God called me to go to Mississippi to care for my Mother. The flights had been perfectly timed as only God could do. My faith in Christ's power and love soared, and I knew I had been part of something wonderful!! I was amazed that He had worked so dramatically in my Mother's life to bring her into relationship with Him.

I began working on this book a few days later, but would occasionally stop work on it as my life began to return to some semblance of normalcy. I taught Bible classes, enjoyed time with my granddaughters and their parents, spent quality time with my husband, and continued one of my pleasures – browsing in Christian bookstores. One day, I went into my favorite bookstore and was alarmed to see what, in my opinion, was a New Age book, *Jesus Calling*, on the shelves masquerading as a Christian book. In the past year, I had spoken to the manager to alert her regarding the clear deception in *God Calling*, as discussed earlier. The manager understood my concern and removed *God Calling* from the bookshelves. However, on this visit I was distressed by the display of *Jesus Calling*, which to me, had a clear association with

God Calling. For example, it was no coincidence that the books have similar titles.

As I drove home, I wept for the Christians and the seekers of Christ who would be misled by this book, and who might accept the full deception found in *God Calling* and *The Course in Miracles*. Acceptance of false doctrine is a slippery slope with one fence relaxed after the next. My heart ached as I cried out to God, and once again felt the Holy Spirit's urging to resume the task of writing this book. I saw my story as one I needed to write, in obedience to Christ. If He used my experiences to turn just one person back from the lies and deception of unbiblical theology, then it was worth the effort. I perceived that as a result of my unique background, I had a "key" to this deception that others without my background would not necessarily appreciate or understand. I felt compelled to tell my story to protect others from falling into the same distortions, falsehoods, and mixed messages that had for a time taken me captive by the great deceiver.

This danger abounds as many Christians are being blindly sucked into this vortex of lies. The leaders do not have to mask their theology because many Christians are not totally aware of the tenets of their own faith. The half-truths combining Scripture and New Age philosophy often deceive believers in Christ and entice them to turn away from sound, biblical orthodoxy. Interestingly, the primary deceiver is not the leader of the movement or the author of the book, but rather the Prince of Darkness himself, the ruler of this world, and the accuser of the brethren, who is "the serpent of old, who is called the devil, and Satan, who deceives the whole world" (Rev. 12:9).

Brooks Alexander analyzes the biblical concerns regarding these spiritistic messages:

> Nearly all spirit communications reiterate the serpent's lie of Genesis 3:4, "you will not surely die." The thrust of most spirit messages is to deny the reality of death and its function as judgment. Now, the Bible implies that judgment is a spur to conscience, which convicts us of sin and leads us to our need for repentance and redemption. If death's spur of judgment is disarmed, then conscience becomes dormant

> and insensitive. Finally, redemption makes no sense, repentance appears irrelevant, and salvation seems to have no meaning. That is precisely the demonic message. It is remarkable for its persistence and consistency in history and its coherence and pervasiveness today. It is no wonder, then, that spiritism provokes rejection and the judgment of God. Everything about it declares that it is at odds with reality and ultimately cannot endure.[40]

The Course in Miracles, God Calling and *Jesus Calling* are not the only deceptive books on Christian bookstore shelves today. In addition to *Jesus Calling,* penned by Sarah Young in 2004, there are also *Jesus Calling* devotionals for teens and kids. More recent books also authored by Sarah Young and published by Thomas Nelson, have followed *Jesus Calling,* including *Dear Jesus*[41] in 2007, *Nearer to Jesus*[42] in 2008, *Jesus Lives*[43] in 2009, and *Jesus Today*[44] in 2012.

I understand the need for encouragement and affirmation, and I too longed to have an intimate touch with God. In my own honest and vulnerable desire to know God better, I was led astray for a time. Spiritual intimacy is exactly what these books promise. They are written in the first person as though Jesus is speaking directly to the reader. The text begins by using Scriptural themes, which gradually progress to Universalist themes, as in the case of *God Calling,* until they finally deny the Christ who made the atonement for us.

Jesus Calling is even more difficult for the Christian to discern the deception because it is written by a former missionary, with a degree in philosophy from Wellesley College, a counseling degree from Georgia State University, a master's degree from Tufts

---

40 Alexander 7.

41 Young, Sarah. *Dear Jesus, Seeking His Life in Your Life.* Nashville, TN: Thomas Nelson, 2007.

42 Young, Sarah. *Nearer to Jesus.* Nashville, TN: Thomas Nelson, 2008.

43 Young, Sarah. *Jesus Lives, Seeing His Love in Your Life.* Nashville, TN: Thomas Nelson, 2009.

44 Young, Sarah. *Jesus Today, Experiencing Hope through His Presence.* Nashville, TN: Thomas Nelson, 2012.

University, and a seminary degree from Covenant Theological Seminary. In addition, the author, Sarah Young, and her husband have traveled around the world with a counseling and church-planting ministry, and now serve in a Japanese-speaking community near Perth in Western Australia. *Jesus Calling* is based on the same practices of the two listeners in *God Calling*, but the academic pedigree of the author has made the errors more difficult to acknowledge and made the book easier for many Christians to accept.

Once again, I acknowledge that Ms Young may have good motives and a pure heart to please God in her writings. I am addressing only the process she used to obtain her text. Unfortunately, Ms Young, though extremely popular, is inadvertently following the wrong spirit in her *Jesus Calling* series. In her introduction, she states that she yearned for more than what God communicated to her through the Bible and determined to use the same technique to approach God as used by the two listeners in *God Calling*. Using Ms Young's words from the introduction to her book:

> During that same year (1992), **I began reading *God Calling*, a devotional book written by two anonymous "listeners." These women practiced waiting quietly in God's Presence, pencils and paper in hand, recording the messages they received from Him.** The messages are written in first person, with "I" designating God. . . . **I began to wonder if I, too, could receive messages** during my times of communing with God. I had been writing in prayer journals for years, but that was one-way communication: I did all the talking. I knew that God communicated with me through the Bible, **but I yearned for more.** Increasingly, **I wanted to hear what God had to say to me personally** on a given day. **I decided to listen to God with pen in hand, writing down whatever I believed He was saying.**[45]

If readers are not familiar with *God Calling* or of the origin of its writings and the heresy that is contained within, then one could easily think Sarah Young is doing a noble thing. We as

[45] Young Introduction X, XI.

Christians have often been told to 'listen to God,' but listening to God with pen in hand for a personal message is very different than listening to God with the Bible in hand. Understanding the process can help to clarify the issues.

Another interesting connection with *God Calling* is Sarah Young's use of the same illustration that is used in the June 10 entry of *God Calling,* in her January 10 entry of *Jesus Calling.* This remarkable coincidence reveals the close alignment of the two books. Both entries establish and support a works-based faith and represent additional information to the biblical text.

> **God Calling, June 10:** *To praise and thank and steadily fulfill your promises (vows) to Me are then, as it were, the placing of coin in My Bank, upon which, in your time of need, you can draw with confidence and certainty. Remember that. The world wonders when it sees the man who can so unexpectedly draw large and unsuspected sums from his bank for his own need, that of a friend, or for some charity. But what the world has not seen are the countless small sums paid into that bank, earned by faithful work in many ways. And so in My Kingdom. The world sees the man of faith make a sudden demand upon Me, upon My stores, and lo! that demand is met. The world thinks the man has magic power – No! the world does not see that the man has been paying in, in thanks and praise, promises fulfilled—faithfully, steadily. So with you, My children. "Offer to God the sacrifice of Thanksgiving and pay your vows to the Most High and call upon Me in the day of trouble and I will deliver you." This is a promise for the seemingly dull days of little happenings, and a cheer for you, My children. When you seem not able to do big things you can be storing your little acts and words of faithfulness in My Great Storehouse, ready for the day of your big demand.*[46]

Obviously, this is extra biblical material from the pages of *God Calling.* Compare that entry to the strikingly similar entry on January 10 in *Jesus Calling*:

> *Every time you affirm your trust in Me, you put a coin into My treasury. Thus you build up equity in preparation for*

[46] Russell June 10.

days of trouble. I keep safely in My heart all trust invested in Me, with interest compounded continuously. The more you trust Me, the more I empower you to do so. Practice trusting Me during quiet days, when nothing much seems to be happening. Then when storms come, your trust balance will be sufficient to see you through. Store up for yourself treasure in heaven, through placing your trust in Me. This practice will keep you in My Peace.[47]

Although Ms Young and the two listeners state that their writings are not equal to Scripture, they belie this assertion by their admission that Jesus is speaking directly to them in a fresh, new revelation. Those who are knowledgeable of New Age practices call what Sarah Young and the two listeners engaged in *automatic writing* (which I had also practiced). I reiterate, in this practice one sits with pen, paper and a receptive mind, empty of all cognitive thought, and then begins to write, without conscious thought, the words and concepts being 'heard.' This passive state allows for an entity to influence or, for the unbeliever, enter the host's body, bypassing the mind and thought processes, and to write a communication via spirit control, as in the Ouija Board practice mentioned earlier. This is the procedure Sarah Young, the two listeners, and Helen Schucman (*The Course in Miracles*) used in their respective publications. This is, in actuality, a form of channeling with the author, knowingly or unknowingly assuming the role of a medium. The genesis of these books speaks clearly of their deceptive roots. Their content is equally suspect.

Unlike *God Calling*, which contains many obvious theological errors, the content of *Jesus Calling* is not as replete with error. There are statements that harmonize with what the Bible teaches, but there are also some troubling parts. Though there are references to Scripture included at the bottom of each page, no verses are written out on the pages of the devotional, nor are readers encouraged to read Scripture. Robert King, *A Christian Rebuttal to Sarah Young's Jesus Calling*,[48] states that the "daily

[47] Young, January 10.

[48] King, Robert A. *A Christian Rebuttal to Sarah Young's "Jesus Calling."* King &Associates, Casa Grande, AZ, 2011. 11.

readings are strikingly similar to a daily horoscope rather than a devotional book." He mentions a few examples that sound very much like a medium's psychic reading:

> The way just ahead of you is very steep. Slow down and cling tightly to My hand. I am teaching you a difficult lesson, learned only by hardship (pg. 39)

> You have journeyed up a steep rugged path in recent days. The way ahead is shrouded in uncertainty (pg. 186).

> You are feeling wobbly this morning, looking at difficult times looming ahead, measuring them against your own strength (pg. 277).

Other statements that are disturbing are the ones that denigrate sin. Ms Young states that "even your mistakes and sins can be recycled into something good through my transforming grace."[49] The consequences for sin are great and should never be taken lightly. Adam and Eve's sin brought the fall of the human race. David's murder of Uriah and sin with Bathsheba (2 Sam. 12) cost David not only the life of his child, but also the consequence of four of his children rising up against him. These were serious consequences that cannot in any way be called trifling or something God uses for good. This misapplication of Romans 8:28 is contrary to biblical teaching. *Even though sometimes those consequences may not be recognized, the consequences do take place. Sin always and in every case will result in damage to the Christian's life and it will not ever work together for good simply because you are a Christian. . . . (This is a) heresy that Satan would love Christians to believe.*[50]

This unholy mix of Christian terms and phrases with New Age philosophy, as evidenced readily in *The Course in Miracles,* as well as in *God Calling,* and its progeny, *Jesus Calling,* can be condensed into three statements:

---

[49] Young 105.

[50] King 6.

1. **Each volume presents itself as an additional, more current and relevant message from God, thereby replacing or adding to the Bible as the authoritative revelation of God.**

Revelation 22:18-20 *I testify to everyone who hears the words of the prophecy of this book: if anyone adds to them, God will add to him the plagues which are written in this book; and if anyone takes away from the words of the book of this prophecy, God will take away his part from the tree of life and from the holy city, which are written in this book. He who testifies to these things says, "Yes, I am coming quickly." Amen. Come, Lord Jesus.*

Charles Spurgeon states the issue clearly:

> The canon of revelation is closed; there is no more to be added; God does not give a fresh revelation, but He rivets the old one. When it has been forgotten, and laid in the dusty chamber of our memory, He fetches it out and cleans the picture, but does not paint a new one. There are no new doctrines, but the old ones are often revived. It is not, I say, by any new revelation that the Spirit comforts. He does so by telling us old things over again; He brings a fresh lamp to manifest the treasures hidden in Scripture; He unlocks the strong chests in which the truth has long lain, and He points to secret chambers filled with untold riches; but He coins no more, for enough is done. Believer! There is enough in the Bible for thee to live upon forever. If thou shouldst outnumber the years of Methuselah, there would be no need for a fresh revelation; if thou shouldst live till Christ should come upon the earth, there would be no necessity for the addition of a single word; if thou shouldst go down as deep as Jonah, or even descend as David said he did, into the belly of hell, still there would be enough in the Bible to comfort thee without a supplementary sentence.[51]

[51] Spurgeon, C.H. *Spurgeon's Gems.* Grand Rapids, MI, Baker Book House, 1980, 61.

2. The message dilutes the perverse nature of sin, calling it a simple mistake, and ignores the cross as the remedy for man's egregious sin condition.

2 Peter 2:1 *But false prophets also arose among the people, just as there will also be false teachers among you, who will secretly introduce destructive heresies, even denying the Master who bought them, bringing swift destruction upon themselves.*

3. The books are dictated, or channeled, by a spirit-guide posing as Jesus.

Galatians 1:8-9 *But even if we, or an angel from heaven, should preach to you a gospel contrary to what we have preached to you, he is to be accursed! As we have said before, so I say again now, if any man is preaching to you a gospel contrary to what you received, he is to be accursed!*

Speaking in the first person, as 'Jesus' addresses the reader in these books, is not some new devotional or literary style, but is a deceptive work channeled by the Father of Lies. The text may seem biblical and the authors may be sincere, but the true author has used these women to pen his deceiving manuscripts to woo even the elect from the truth. One can be sincere and be sincerely wrong.

As I emphasized before, this practice is called automatic writing. That alone should drive believers in the true God to discard these books and renounce the teachings they contain. Although the content may not be totally anti-biblical, the source is, and it is a slippery slope to total apostasy when the source is tainted. *A little yeast works through the whole batch of dough* (Gal. 5:9 NIV). The one posing as the angel of light will in time reveal his true colors.

It is heart breaking that many of the flock of the Lord have been so seduced by the enemy of our souls. I wonder how many will pick up this new packaging of an old craft and attempt to also receive messages from 'Jesus.' How many of our children will be led astray by the lies the enemy sells them through their honest desire for spiritual intimacy? Who will channel the next 'devotional' and gradually slip from the truth to the lie of universalism (all good people will go to heaven) and deny the necessity of the cross to cleanse and cover the sins of those who receive Jesus??

These three points are the major concerns that should raise red flags in the hearts and minds of God's people. These books stand like wolves in sheep's clothing trying to woo the sheep away from the shepherd by their similar sounding words and unholy mix of Scripture with worldly philosophies and false teachings. An increasing number of Christians are being *sucked into this whirlpool of spiritual confusion in which they exchange the truth for a lie.*[52] The promised intimacy with this new 'Jesus,' as presented in these devotionals and in the broader work of *The Course in Miracles,* has seduced more Christians away from the Bible and deceived them with comforting words combined with a splash of Scripture, which is often taken out of context and misapplied, so as to lead even the elect astray. By mixing a small amount of the truth with the lies, the lies are made far stronger.[53] But Truth and lies are not compatible. As believers in Christ, we have an obligation to expose these deeds of darkness (Eph. 5:6-14), so that others will not slip into the same pits from which we have been fortunate to escape.

If you are a Christian and have fallen for the enemy's lies, as I did, and are feeling ashamed that you were duped and led astray, then know that *there is no condemnation for those who are in Christ Jesus* (Rom. 8:1). The Lord wants to restore you, not condemn you.

Ephesians 5:6–14 *Let no one deceive you with empty words, for because of these things the wrath of God comes upon the sons of disobedience. Therefore do not be partakers with them; for you were formerly darkness, but now you are Light in the Lord; walk as children of Light (for the fruit of the Light consists in all goodness and righteousness and truth), trying to learn what is pleasing to the Lord. Do not participate in*

---

[52] Wise, Russ. "A Course in Miracles. "Probe Ministries 1996: n. pag. Web. 29 April 2012.

[53] Lewis, C.S. *The Last Battle.* HarperCollins Pub., NY. 1984. 116.

the unfruitful deeds of darkness, but instead even expose them; for it is disgraceful even to speak of the things which are done by them in secret. But all things become visible when they are exposed by the light, for everything that becomes visible is light. For this reason it says,

"Awake, sleeper,
and arise from the dead,
and Christ will shine on you."

A Brief Comparison of *The Course in Miracles*, *God Calling*, *Jesus Calling*, and the *Bible*

	The Course in Miracles[54]	God Calling[55]	Jesus Calling[56]	The Bible
Author	Helen Schucman, atheistic psychologist	Two Anonymous Listeners from England	Sarah Young	God led approximately 40 human authors so that, while using their own writing styles and personalities, they wrote exactly what God intended. The Bible was not dictated by God, but was uniquely guided and totally inspired by Him.
Method Received	Dictation via automatic writing through the same method employed by a medium or channeler	Dictation via automatic writing through the method employed by a medium or channeler	Dictation via automatic writing through the same method employed by a medium or channeler	*. . . for no prophecy was ever made by an act of human will, but men moved by the Holy Spirit spoke from God.* 2 Peter 1:21
Who Transmitted	Spiritistic literature dictated by a guide believed to be "Jesus"	Spiritistic literature dictated by a guide believed to be "the Living Christ Himself" *So to us this book, which we believe has been guided by our Lord Himself, is no ordinary book* ("The Voice Devine," Introduction by one of the "Two Listeners").	Spiritistic literature dictated by a guide believed to be "Jesus" (pg.XI, Introduction) *Each day is written as if Jesus Himself were speaking to you. Because He is. Do you hear Him calling?* (Back book cover)	*All Scripture is inspired by God and profitable for teaching, for reproof, for correction, for training in righteousness; so that the man of God may be adequate, equipped for every good work.* 2 Timothy 3:16–17

	The Course in Miracles[54]	God Calling[55]	Jesus Calling[56]	The Bible
Description	Daily New Age occult devotional published in 1975	Daily devotional published in mid to late 1930's; channeled in 1932-33	Daily devotional published in 2004	*A collection of books, accepted by the Christian church as uniquely inspired by God, and thus authoritative, providing guidelines for belief and behavior.*[57]
Major Goal	*Mental attitudes are gradually restructured to harmonize with a New Age spiritistic worldview* (pg. 1)	*We felt all unworthy and overwhelmed by the wonder of it, and could hardly realize that we were being taught, trained, and encouraged by HIM personally, when millions of souls, far worthier, had to be content with guidance from the Bible, sermons, their churches, books and other sources* ("The Voice Devine").	*During that same year (1992), I began reading* ***God Calling****.... The following year, I began to wonder if I, too, could receive messages during my times of communing with God... I knew that God communicated with me through the Bible, but I yearned for more. ....I decided to listen to God with pen in hand, writing down whatever I believed He was saying* (pg. XI).	*But the goal of our instruction is love from a pure heart and a good conscience and a sincere faith.* 1 Timothy 1:5

[54] Ankerberg, John and John Weldon, *Encyclopedia of New Age Beliefs.* Eugene, OR: Harvest House, 1996, 1-2.

[55] Russell, A.J., ed. *God Calling.* Uhrichsville, OH: Barbour Publishing, Inc., 1989.

[56] Young, Sarah. *Jesus Calling, Enjoying Peace in His Presence.* Nashville, TN: Thomas Nelson, 2004. (Introduction).

[57] *Nelson's New Illustrated Bible Dictionary,* ed. Ronald F. Youngblood, F. F. Bruce, R. K. Harrison and Thomas Nelson Publishers. Nashville, TN: Thomas Nelson, Inc., 1995.

	The Course in Miracles[54]	God Calling[55]	Jesus Calling[56]	The Bible
Evaluation of False Teaching	*The Bible teaches the opposite of what the Course teaches on almost every subject* (pg. 1).	*The text denies the atonement (pg. 157, 216), subtly encourages psychic development and spiritistic inspiration under the guise of Christ's personal guidance (pg. 44-45, 55-56, 117-18, etc.) and misinterprets Scripture (pg. 56).*[58]	The book does not represent total error. There are statements that harmonize with what the Bible teaches, but there are also distortions of the character of God, use of Scripture out of context, and an avoidance of the problem of personal sin and Christ's efficacious, atoning death on the cross.	*But the Spirit explicitly says that in later times some will fall away from the faith, paying attention to deceitful spirits and doctrines of demons, . . .* 1 Timothy 4:1
Example of False Teaching	*The Course teaches that everyone is a worker of miracles and a spiritual healer. The basic purpose of these" miracles" is to unlearn orthodox Christianity, especially the belief in Christ's atonement for sin (pg. 1-2).*	*See me in the dull, the uninteresting, the sinful, the critical, the miserable* (Jun 30). *So only I, being God, can recognize the God in Man* (May 14). *I need you more than you need me* (Mar. 29). *I await the commands of my children* (Apr 3) (pg. 103-104).	Conversion is represented by a warm feeling and whispering "Sweet Jesus" instead of through repentance and forgiveness of sin found in the shed blood of Jesus Christ on the cross (pg. VII). Sarah Young is telling the reader what God told her. Regardless of how much Scripture she uses, she is putting herself in the position of speaking to the reader the very words of God. *I have continued to receive personal messages from God . . .* (pg. XI).	*But evil men and impostors will proceed from bad to worse, deceiving and being deceived.* 2 Timothy 3:13 *For such men are false apostles, deceitful workers, disguising themselves as apostles of Christ. No wonder, for even Satan disguises himself as an angel of light.* 2 Corinthians 11:13–14 *Be diligent to present yourself approved to God as a workman who does not need to be ashamed, accurately handling the word of truth.* 2 Timothy 2:15

	The Course in Miracles[54]	God Calling[55]	Jesus Calling[56]	The Bible
Potential Danger	*The adopting of occult philosophy and practice in the guise of physical, mental, and spiritual enlightenment . . .* (pg. 2)	Deception by the evil one and the slow absorption of New Age thought in a semi biblical cloak. It implies that personal guidance is more acceptable than the Bible and puts forth additional words from the mouth of Christ.	The acceptance of an additional work to the Bible that is touted to be more current, readable and relational than Scripture	*I testify to everyone who hears the words of the prophecy of this book: if anyone adds to them, God will add to him the plagues which are written in this book.* Revelation 22:18

Biblical Evaluation	Material comprises occult revelations from a medium, which is expressly forbidden in the Bible. *There shall not be found among you anyone who makes his son or his daughter pass through the fire, one who uses divination, one who practices witchcraft, or one who interprets omens, or a sorcerer, or one who casts a spell, or a medium, or a spiritist, or one who calls up the dead. For whoever does these things is detestable to the Lord; and because of these detestable things the Lord your God will drive them out before you.* Deuteronomy 18:9-12

[58] Ankerberg, *Encyclopedia of New Age Beliefs*, 103- 104, referencing: Russell, A.J., ed. *God Calling*. NY: Dodd, Mead & Co., 1945, with page numbers.

X
JOURNEY TO THE END

Now, I'm telling the world your wonders;
I'll keep at it until I'm old and gray.
Psalm 71:18 (TM)

After the hospital stay and before departing for Virginia, Mother and I frequently prayed together. She talked to God herself and prayed that her friend would find a church and experience the peace that she had found. I was ecstatic! At long last my heart's desire had been realized. Years of prayer and waiting, persevering in hope and trusting God had finally given birth to my 'Isaac.' My joy was overwhelming as I identified with Abraham and Sarah's laughter after long years of waiting for the birth of their promised child! But my bliss was to be short lived.

I would love to say that Mother's last days were sweet and alive with the nearness of God, but that is not what we experienced. Dementia symptoms increased with personality changes, inappropriate behavior, and agitation. The last year of Mother's life was perplexing as we saw our loved-one experiencing some radical changes as a result of her medical condition.

Mom's year since the Great Miracle was full of activity. Two of her brothers passed away and Mary took Mother to both funerals in the Kansas City area, even combining a delightful camping trip along the way. In September, the family gathered in Wichita, KS, to celebrate the 80th birthday of Mother and her fraternal twin sister. We were all surprised to see the marked difference in the health of Mother, who was weak and struggled with breathing and walking, as opposed to her twin sister, who was strong and looked at least 15 years younger than Mother.

During those trips, Mary had opportunities to speak in a loving and gentle way of Christ as their conversations touched upon Him. Their journeys were a highlight for Mom, as Mary served Mother to the end as though she were serving Christ Himself. Mary's husband, Jeff, was also a favorite of Mom's, especially as he lifted and carried her to her bed during her days of decreasing mobility, and performed other feats of mercy that involved strength. Mom loved feeling like a princess when Jeff carried her.

In the past, Jeff and Mary had been Mother's 'go to' people when she had a project. Most of the projects they accomplished for her should have been done by professionals, but Jeff and Mary were available and eager to help Mom do what she desired. Mom's landscaping projects were the ideas of a skilled artist and planner who could no longer lift and carry heavy loads to realize her dreams, but she knew just how each project should be accomplished. Jeff and Mary lived within a few hours from Mom, and both of them dedicated their time, strength, and weekends to helping Mother bring about her landscaping schemes, inasmuch as they were able. They incurred repeated poison ivy infections and other physical pains and injuries as a result of their kind service. Having such willing and benevolent helpers made Mom so happy! These sweet and sacrificial gifts created openness in their relationship that allowed my sister to frequently remind Mother of what Christ had done for her. Mary never wasted a word on Mother, as each idea was carefully thought out before it was spoken.

Mom's health continued to decline during the summer and fall of the year. In October 2010, a dear Christian cousin passed away. I flew down to travel to the funeral with Mom and Mary. The funeral was a wonderful proclamation of Christ, and we were all touched by our cousin's godly example. Mother could not stop talking about the funeral. As only God could have arranged it, Mother was seated on the third row in that small funeral parlor so that she could see the speaker and focus on the clear gospel message. Our cousin had known my mother was not a Christian, and though we never discussed this with him or his family, it blessed me to know that they too had been praying for Mother and placed her in the most advantageous seat.

Mother stayed a month in Tennessee with my youngest sister for the latter part of November and the first part of December 2010. That visit was difficult for both of them, but Deb was able to get Mother involved in water therapy. My sister worked full time, so Mother was alone much of the time during the day. Her dementia was becoming more evident without interaction with people, and culminated with a panic attack just before Christmas vacation. Deb was able to start her Christmas vacation from work earlier than planned and Mother's last Christmas was happily spent in Jackson in her own home. She was thrilled to be there again, but her medical issues were increasing. The edema in her legs forced Mother to be hospitalized once again. Medications and treatments were given that seemed to reduce much of the excess fluid and discomfort. Her breathing became shallow and her coloring went from pink to a gray/blue/yellow combo. Finally, a doctor counseled my sister to call in the rest of the family.

Once again, God 'called' the timing of my visit. As I prayed, I felt His leading to purchase a ticket for Sunday, January 3, 2011. My flight was scheduled to leave early from Baltimore, but upon arriving at the airport terminal, I was surprised to see that the check-in line ran past the check-in queue line, the luggage security check, the personal security check area, the bathrooms, around the back of the escalators and then back toward the entrance of the queue line. Even with one hour before my flight, this looked impossible. We began to think of ways to 'fix' the problem…leave my luggage and just go with my carry on, etc. Finally, I remembered 1 Thessalonians 5:24, "Faithful is He who calls you and He will also bring it to pass." I avowed my faith and waited. Before I made it in the line to the front of the bathrooms, an airline representative came by saying, "If you have printed boarding passes, join this line." I DID and was at my gate moments before boarding was called. Even my late checked luggage made the flight. This beginning of the trip reminded me that I was on a God-errand, as well as off to bid my mother farewell.

I arrived in Jackson and went directly to the hospital to visit my mother. Though weak, she appeared to rally, thus giving me hope for recovery. I reminded myself that God is able to accomplish more than we ask or think.

The hospital time was spent serving and embracing Mom. During my night duty, I read Scripture from 1 John, Revelation, and Psalms out loud. While there, I had a sense of purpose, and during time at home, I was able to get ample rest, making me a better warrior on night duty.

When I had night duty, I spent my waking hours praying and engaging in spiritual warfare for her, as well as assisting with her numerous needs. I loved this time the best – watching her sleep and perceiving myself as standing guard over her bed, along with the heavenly host. One evening, Mother was served a new drug, which caused her to sleep for two days. I felt cheated of the little amount of time we had left, and requested that the drug be stopped. Other drugs were given in an attempt to manage her anxiety and sleeplessness.

The Social Worker and Hospice were called in, but I held on to the hope that she would rally again. I clung to that hope until we got home, where I saw Mother continuing to lose ground without regaining her former strength. At that time, I grieved as I witnessed her slow, but continuous decline.

XI
THE FINAL WEEK

You keep me going when times are tough, my bedrock, God, since my childhood.
Psalm 71:5 (TM)

My sister, Mary, and I decided to facilitate home hospice for Mom so that she could remain in her home in a comfortable environment. We had no idea how hard that would be without the help of the nurses and the change in shifts. We took turns with 24-hour duty, and we each dealt with the progression of Mom's dementia and her anxious and sleepless nights. These duty nights were the hardest for me, and I quickly began to lose my perspective as to why I was there and what my purpose and goal were. I so wanted to rejoice and give thanks for the gift God gave us in allowing us to, in a sense, 'walk Mom to the very gate of heaven,' to be present with her as she took her last breath on earth and had her first glimpse of the Savior.... and sometimes I did rejoice. Other times, I complained of her jelly legs (though small, her body weight was still too much for me to lift) and her constant ingratitude. In retrospect, I am ashamed of my un-Christlike behavior and attitude during Mom's last days. Lack of sleep and the incessant demands and emotional assaults often left me incapable of a good response. The insanity around me was more than I could comprehend with my own unique wiring where right is right, without deviation. With Mother, we were in an exclusive cocoon of insanity. She did not sleep at all, which also prevented us, as her caretakers, from sleeping. In addition, her attention-getting antics and childlike behavior belied her normally more serious demeanor. To see Mother acting in such a contradictory way was disconcerting. I was at a loss to comprehend the changes and was emotionally spent as I sought to serve one who, at times, seemingly appreciated it so little. In a few words, I was quickly exhausted by the challenges we were presented.

At one point in response to a barrage of her constant demands and complaints, I stated that, "My mother taught me to say please and thank you". She grimaced, but later incorporated a few polite words in her requests. When I mentioned her ingratitude, the Holy Spirit came quickly to convict my heart of my own ingratitude. As I helped Mom stand, she clung to me in a standing hug and I whispered in her ear that I had been the ungrateful one. I asked her to forgive me. We laughed and hugged…and enjoyed the last sweet embrace in which she was lucid and truly responsive to me.

Mother engaged in specific antics during those days at home. When family would come to visit and would be talking with my sister and me in another room, Mom began to 'fall out of bed.' As I saw her do it later, she actually would move her hand to touch the floor and then slide down to the floor from her bed. Of course, we would discover her on the floor and be upset that Mom had 'fallen' out of the bed. One time, as she performed this acrobatic feat, she actually slipped and her head hit the trash can. We all laughed so hard as we talked about Mom's head in the trash can! Even she had a wonderful giggle from the event. Other than the trash can incident, Mother was never hurt by her 'falls.'

Another health concern was regarding Mother's sitting on the side of the bed with her feet down. We had such a battle to keep her feet up so as to prevent the fluid from pooling in her feet. Once the fluid was present, it would be a battle to get rid of it before it did more harm to Mother's ailing and weak heart. The hospital bed appeared to be our answer and the hospice team acted quickly so that we had the bed on the same day that it was requested.

Though I knew on some level that we were still in spiritual warfare, I lost my focus rapidly. Lack of sleep and intense emotional strain caused me to forget my mission and my calling.

Knowing that hospice could last several weeks or months, I was still open to doing anything that God asked me/us to do. I could not have guessed that the time that remained for Mom was so short. I am sure I was in denial.

Journal Entry:
Monday, January 10, 2011

. . .All went well with getting the king sized bed out of Mom's room and setting up the hospital bed. Mom should not be falling out of bed anymore and her care should be easier. She is more captive and her feet are contained in the bed so our fight to keep her feet up is over. We had her up in the living room a bit. She also ate her meals with us at the table. She seems to be getting better...or at least not getting worse. Judy (my sister-in-law*) came over and prayed for her. We also skyped with the family at home. Beka* (my eldest daughter who had flown down to Mississippi with her 2 yr. old daughter to be a help in these final days*) and I ran a few errands to get out of the house. It is sleeting here.*

Today, as I look into Your Word...grant me meat...not just empty calories to confuse my soul or to give me false hope. Please give me meat and potatoes and vegetables for greater growth and faith. I need YOU for the living of today. I put my faith completely in You. Please encourage my spirit.

Kay (my youngest daughter) *sent snippets from Beth Moore to encourage us.* (Beth Moore is a well-known Bible teacher who also has a daily blog)

"How thankful I am for the freedom God has increasingly given me in Christ. I'm in the throes of middle age-(as one of my friends says "time is a great healer but a lousy beautician")-yet I am happier and more satisfied than I've ever been. The secret? I'm learning to see myself as beautiful in Christ.

Without Christ, every woman has intense insecurities. Unless we find our identity in Him, we Christian women can be just as prone to insecurities about our appearance as unbelievers. ***To Christ, the most***

beautiful person on earth is the one making preparation to meet the Groom."[59]

Lord, I so love You, my Holy Groom. Mom, too, is coming Your way . . . Lord, make her beautiful to You as You craft her into a woman of God. I surrender all to You this morning...my hopes, dreams, desires...all to You to make them into a reality that gives glory to Your name, in Your timing.

Hebrews 10:36 But you need to stick it out, staying with God's plan so you'll be there for the promised completion. (TM)

Hebrews 10:36 *For ye have need of* **patience**, *that, after ye have done the will of God, ye might receive the promise.* ***(KJ)***

Hebrews 10:36 *For you have need of* ***endurance, so that when you have done the will of God, you may receive what was promised. (NASB95)***

THERE!! That is MEAT for what faces me today!! YES!! I am holding on!
Fear and doubt are conquered by a faith that rejoices. *Help me stick it out, endure, and be patient in my circumstances. I am rejoicing in You today...please grant me genuine joy and not fake and surface stuff... genuine love and a genuine focus on You. I love You, Lord.*

2 Chronicles 20: 12 *"O our God, will You not judge them? For* ***we are powerless before this great multitude who are coming against us; nor do we know what to do, but our eyes are on You."***

YOU have given me hope!! Thank You for speaking directly to my heart through Your word. . . . Thanks for Your kindness to meet me this morning. Carry us through the day. Grant us all joy and increase our faith... please encourage us today.

---

[59] Moore, Beth. *Breaking Free Day by Day.* B&H Publishing Group: Nashville, TN, 2007, January 6.

Journal Entry:
Wednesday, January 12, 2011

"There is a balance to be maintained in situations. That balance is ***the Holy Spirit within us to guide us into the truth of each situation and circumstance in which we find ourselves. He will provide us the wisdom to know when we are to be adaptable and adjustable and when we are to take a firm stand and be immovable."*** *Joyce Meyer*[60]

Luke 23 and 24 - Lord, Your resurrection was so glorious, yet even Your disciples did not recognize it as coming from the Scriptures. I too feel like the child...unskilled and awkward. How can I do adult thinking when I am still a child inside? How could they understand the deeper things, when they were still new to this walk? I so need You for today. Help me simply depend on You for help and love.

Hospice nurses and aides helped us with those final days. Even a nun came by to pray with Mother, and Judy, my sister-in-law, who is a Chaplain, also dropped by to pray with her. Mother appeared to respond to both prayers, even with tears, but without any conversation. On the last day, as my sister and I stood by her bed and prayed for her, Mother wanted to sit up in a chair. She took her medication and as I rubbed her feet, I sang hymns to her....*Amazing Grace, Rock of Ages, On Christ the Solid Rock I Stand,* and then one more that I had not sung in a long time came to mind. Mother peacefully listened to the words of the songs and I sensed Mother 'singing' along with me.

Set My Spirit Free to Worship Thee
Set my spirit free to praise Your name.
Let all bondage go and let deliverance flow.
Set my spirit free to worship You.[61]

---

[60] "The Balancing Act". *100 Days of Praise for Women. Family Christian Stories.* Grand Rapids, MI. 2008. 45.

[61] Anonymous

Mom had jelly legs as I tried to put her back in bed. My daughter ran in to help me lift Mother back on the bed. I left Mom to rest and she finally fell asleep, mostly due to the medications given earlier.

I was able to get a short nap, and then I checked on Mom. She slept deeply. I went for a quick walk, praying for strength to make it through the night. I returned and checked on her again. This time I saw saliva on the side of her chin. I wiped it, left, returned and wiped another portion from her chin. Then I began to think something wasn't right. I expected Mom to wake and bat my hand away from her face as I wiped the saliva. The eyes play tricks on the mind at times like this. I actually thought I saw her chest expand with her breathing, then I remembered the movies and went to get a mirror to place under her nose to see if she was breathing. Nothing happened, so I figured this was a worthless test. As I put the mirror up, I finally processed the fact that 'nothing happened'...because she wasn't breathing!! I called my sister and daughter to help me confirm Mother's status. We established that Mom had indeed passed away. We gathered at the head of her bed and thanked God for His kindness to her and to us in providing her as our Mother. We celebrated the fact that now she knew the whole truth and was embracing Jesus and gazing at His holy face. There were no doubts, lies, or deception anymore. She finally KNEW the Truth! Mom had been set free to worship Jesus Christ, the One she invited into her life almost a year ago to the date.

The hospice nurse came and confirmed our findings. Mom had decided earlier to donate her body to science, so within three hours of her death, her body was taken away. At that moment we knew that we had to call our two siblings with the news. My youngest sister, Deb lived alone, five hours away. The thought of calling her and leaving her to grieve alone was unthinkable. Mary and I jumped in the car and drove the five hours. We turned off the car in the driveway and called our sister on the phone with the news, then added, "Open the garage; we are here to be with you." From there, we made our calls to my brother and other family members and friends, returning to Jackson the next day to complete our tasks.

And so ended my mother's life-struggle. The medications were cleared away and the house was restored to its earlier, pre-hospice condition. A few weeks later, the family gathered in the house again, surrounded by several friends and neighbors, as we celebrated Mother's life. The reality that both of our parents (mother and step-father) were gone began to set in. (My own father died in September of this same year.) Now, we were orphans, devoid of the parental influence that shaped our lives. We were now the generation that would answer to our children for the wounds and sorrows that they experienced in the exercise of our own dysfunction. Each generation takes its turn. It is my prayer that the filial damage will be less debilitating as each generation in our family steps up to take the helm from the previous generation.

I am thankful for the heritage I have been given, knowing that God made no mistake in placing me in my parents' care. The strengths and weaknesses I learned in my childhood formed the character I now possess. I am also grateful that, after mercifully bringing me to Himself, God gave me a spiritual longing for my parents and siblings to come to know and love Jesus Christ as well. This longing resulted in many prayers on their behalf, and in the process, I experienced a greater faith and increasing trust in the God who finally brought the answer about in such a majestic and powerful way. I stand in awe of Him, and I steadfastly await the answers to my fervent prayers for my other siblings.

One character trait I acquired through the years is a tenacious clinging to the truths found in the Bible. I spent many years identifying the lies and deception in my own thinking and have a protective care for those who are less capable of distinguishing those same mixed messages. I began by protecting my daughters from the false teaching of my mother, and now I have a burden to protect others who are less informed of the New Age practices. This desire to guard the gospel message led to the writing of this book, which was my next courageous, albeit sometimes frightening, step of faith.

XII
THE GRAND ADVENTURE

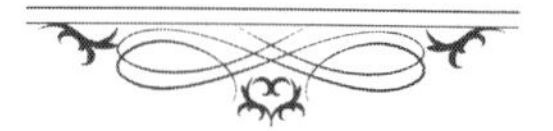

*When I open up in song to you, I let out lungs full of praise,
my rescued life a song.
Psalm 71:23 (TM)*

This adventure began for me with a simple heartfelt cry for help when I asked God to be the Rescuer of my life back in 1974. I knew the reality of Colossians 1:13–14, which states that, *He rescued us from the domain of darkness, and transferred us to the kingdom of His beloved Son, in whom we have redemption, the forgiveness of sins.* From the time of my awareness of the reality of Christ, I fervently prayed for my mother to receive Jesus as her Rescuer, as well. Years passed and I continued to hold on to the hope that Mother would surrender her whole heart to Him. Only He could have arranged the spectacular events that culminated in that moment of faith for my mother. My sister and I witnessed the answer to our fervent prayers, which, for me, spanned over 36 years. God never missed a single tear I wept on her behalf, nor turned a deaf ear to a single prayer whispered from my heart, or from my sister's heart. Through the years, I clung to words from the Scriptures that gave me hope, and I used those very words to pray back to Him on her behalf. No magic formula, just words from the heart. His answer was as tremendous and as beautiful as the wait was long, but it was no less a miracle, a testimony of His great power and grace. Whether, by strict definition, one would call the culmination of this series of happenings that God used to orchestrate His will in my mother's life a miracle or not, one cannot deny the work of God in the midst of it. Untold events and people were inserted in her life with the goal of wooing her to Himself. This love story ended in a wonderful shout of GLORY to the One who orchestrated it all simply because He loved her. It was certainly worth the delay to have the display of His glory.

If you too see yourself as lost or separated from God, needing to be reconciled to Him, be assured that the Good Shepherd will leave a flock of ninety and nine to rescue one lamb that has lost its way (Luke 15:4). You are so much more valuable than an animal. Jesus, the Good Shepherd actually died for you so that you could have your sins, your wrong and willful acts of rebellion against God's rule in your life, forgiven and be with him in heaven some day. Jesus' death paid the penalty for all your sins and you can be forgiven by trusting and believing that He did what He said He would do on your behalf. His sacrifice atones for your sin and His salvation is applied to you when you confess your trust in Him. He says that *if we confess with our mouths Jesus as Lord and believe in our hearts that God raised Jesus from the dead, we will be saved. For with our hearts, we believe and become righteous, and with our mouths we confess Him and receive salvation* (Romans 10:9-10).

Our relationship with Christ is much like a marriage. The wedding ceremony is only the beginning of that lifetime commitment to share all of life's choices and experiences together. The engagement period is the initial discovery stage, but the wedding commitment is a lifetime decision. Time is spent in getting to know the personality and character of one another and love blossoms into a deep friendship. One would not want to be stuck in the engagement period too long, yet sometimes that happens in our experience. Sometimes we may go to all the right places, do good things and think we are Christians, but until we stand up and say, I DO, as in a marriage ceremony, we are not really His. Don't misunderstand. It is not a formal event like a wedding, but a moment in time in which the heart is bowed and the cry elicited is one from a sincere heart. If you would like to say I DO to Jesus, to invite Him to take control of your life and to lead you into a relationship with Him, you can tell God by saying the words of a simple heartfelt prayer right now. Talk to God; He is listening.

Dear Lord Jesus, I DO believe that You are the Son of God, and that You died on the cross to pay the penalty for my sin. Because of Your atoning sinless sacrifice You rose to life again and will give me a new life just for the asking. I NEED a new life! Please come into my life, forgive my sin and make me a member of Your family. I now turn from going my own way, and I want you to be the center of my life and my Shepherd forever. Thank You for Your gift of eternal life and for Your Holy Spirit, who has now come to live in me. I ask this in Your name. Amen.

Welcome to the family of God, and welcome to the wonderful adventure of falling in love with Jesus! You have stepped into His exquisite and unique love story with yourself as the object of His love. As you grow in your relationship with Him, you will see how He has been wooing and drawing you to Himself since your entrance into this world. How He loves you!! And He has a wonderful plan to direct the remainder of your life! That plan may involve trials, suffering, even persecution, along with joys and blessings indescribable, but He promises that He will never leave, nor forsake you. His goal in your life is to make you more like Him. We are

> no longer to be children, tossed here and there by waves and carried about by every wind of doctrine, by the trickery of men, by craftiness in deceitful scheming; but speaking the truth in love, we are to grow up in all *aspects* into Him who is the head, *even* Christ, from whom the whole body, being fitted and held together by what every joint supplies, according to the proper working of each individual part, causes the growth of the body for the building up of itself in love. Ephesians 4:14–16

This IS the Grand Adventure!! You will fall in love with Him and even this love will pale in comparison to His wonderful love for you. As time passes, you will find that HE, Jesus Christ, is the STAR, or center, of your own life's drama. He provides the strength and desire to obey His commands and He receives the praise, honor, and glory for all that He alone has accomplished in your life. Yes, it IS a Grand Adventure!

As I come to the end of this book, it is my prayer that someone will pick it up and accept the offer of life eternal contained in the pages. Much like my own mother found in the pages of *Same Kind of Different As Me,* may this book be used by God to open the eyes of the blind, *so that they may turn from darkness to light and from the dominion of Satan to God in order that they may receive forgiveness of sins and an inheritance among those who have been sanctified by faith in Me* (Acts 26:18).

My mother and I were ***snatched from the jaws of the lion***. There is no doubt in my mind that my mother is now enjoying The Grand Adventure in heaven. In my sanctified imagination, I imagine my mother gazing lovingly into the eyes of Jesus, then turning back to me and pleading with me to use her life to bring glory to the One who pursued her until her last day.

I am enjoying my Grand Adventure here on earth and look forward to an eternity that greatly exceeds even my imagination. It is my desire that you too will join my mother and me, along with countless other Christians, at the throne of grace, and that you too will enjoy your own Grand Adventure now and forever more. Amen.

I conclude with the words of Paul as he said goodbye to the flock at Ephesus:

Acts 20:24–32 *"But I do not consider my life of any account as dear to myself, so that I may finish my course and the ministry which I received from the Lord Jesus, to testify solemnly of the gospel of the grace of God. And now, behold, I know that all of you, among whom I went about preaching the kingdom, will no longer see my face. Therefore, I testify to you this day that I am innocent of the blood of all men. For I did not shrink from declaring to you the whole purpose of God. Be on guard for yourselves and for all the flock, among which the Holy Spirit has made you overseers, to shepherd the church of God which He purchased with His own blood. I know that after my departure savage wolves will come in among you, not sparing the flock; and from among your own selves men will arise, speaking perverse things, to draw away the disciples after them. Therefore be on the alert, remembering that night and day for a period of three years I did not cease to admonish each one with tears. And* *now I commend you to God and to the word of His grace, which is able to build you up and to give you the inheritance among all those who are sanctified.*

To God be the glory for the great things that only He can do, even with this small, but sincere, offering.

APPENDIX

In this section, I offer a list of helpful resources to facilitate the reader's own investigation into the concerns I have expressed regarding the three books mentioned in Chapter IX of this book. I have given a short critique of each website mentioned and have included the link. Some of the sites are from blogs and others are from organizations. I have used these sources to increase my own understanding of the issues, and it is my hope that you too will find them useful. In addition, I have included information on books or booklets that may be useful in your research.

A Summary Critique: God Calling

This is an excellent book review by Edmond C. Gruss from the Christian Research Journal, Issue 11-01, *Seventh Day Adventism.* The magazine issue is no longer available for purchase, but the article contained within can be viewed online.
http://journal.equip.org/articles/a-summary-critique-god-calling-

Book Review: God Calling edited by A.J. Russell

A strong book review by Dwayna Litz and Charisse Graves, of Lighting the Way International, details the content of the book in light of biblical principles. Be sure to note the mention of *Jesus Calling* in the first paragraph.
http://www.lighthousetrailsresearch.com/blog/?p=3764

God Calling: Is It?

Steven Tsoukalas evaluates the book in a short article which addresses the teachings of *God Calling.* He concludes his article with a heartfelt cry, "Wake Up Church!" His review was published by Sound Doctrine Ministries in the March 2001 edition of *The Sounding Board.*
http://www.sdmin.org/soundingboard/200103.htm

A Christian's Rebuttal to A.J. Russell's and the Two Listeners' God Calling

Robert Alan King presents a 27 page rebuttal to *God Calling,* pointing out specific concerns. It is well worth reading.

His work is available online through Amazon and also through Smashwords Edition, copyright 2011 by King and Associates. Casa Grande, AZ.

Probe Ministries: *A Course in Miracles*

This is an excellent article written by Russ Wise. It is a relatively short work that covers the topic well. Mr. Wise also includes a story of a couple who came out of *The Course in Miracles.*
http://www.probe.org/site/c.fdKEIMNsEoG/b.4217745/k.57D6/A_Course_In_Miracles.htm

A Course in Brainwashing

Tracy Moran addresses the acceptance in the Catholic Church of *The Course in Miracles.* Moran's article was published in the June 2, 1996, edition of *Our Sunday Visitor,* a Catholic publication.
http://www.ewtn.com/library/newage/brainwas.txt

The following publications regarding *The Course in Miracles* are from the Ankerberg Theological Research Institute. The scholarship found in their evaluations and their straight forward approaches to the issues are unequaled.

A Course in Miracles/Attitudinal Therapy, Info at a Glance

This site offers a two page summary of the information contained in the three other works depicted below by Ankerberg.
http://www.ankerberg.com/Articles/_PDFArchives/new-age/NA3W0699.pdf

A Course in Miracles – Part 1, 2, and 3

This information is thorough and well documented. It is an excellent resource to answer all of your questions on the topic.
Part 1: http://www.jashow.org/Articles/new-age/NA0509W1.htm
Part 2: http://www.jashow.org/Articles/_PDFArchives/new-age/NA1W0609.pdf
Part 3:http://www.ankerberg.com/Articles/new-age/NA0709W1.htm

Jesus Calling?, reviewed by Rob Willmann

This short book review was posted on May 27, 2010, by Rendering Truth.com. The website is devoted to, "promoting the Gospel of Jesus Christ, for the glory of God and the furtherance of His Kingdom." The author, Rob Willmann, primarily focuses on Sarah Young's boredom with the Scriptures, her method of transmission, and her writing as from Jesus' perspective.
http://www.renderingtruth.com/2010/05/jesus-calling/

Jesus Calling, reviewed by Tim Challies

Tim Challies looks at the book using two points: "What She Says About What She Says" and "What She Says." He evaluates the author's claim that Jesus is speaking through her and concludes that it is a "very dangerous book." Mr. Challies does not address the New Age aspects of the work, but does offer a review of the devotional book for children, *Jesus Calling: 365 Devotions for Kids.*
http://www.challies.com/book-reviews/jesus-calling
http://www.challies.com/book-reviews/jesus-is-calling-for-kids

Jesus Calling, reviewed by Dr. Stephen Hague

Dr. Hague is the Academic Dean and Professor of Biblical Theology from Faith Theological Seminary. His succinct review addresses Ms Young's writing process and her yearning for more than Scripture to meet her heart's need. He also notes that "the theology of Young's devotional is thin."
http://faiththeological.org/news-events/blog/book-review-on-jesus-calling/

Jesus Calling, reviewed by Dr. Michael Horton

Dr. Michael Horton is the main host of the *White Horse Inn* radio broadcast, and is also Professor of Apologetics and Theology at Westminster Seminary California and editor-in-chief of *Modern Reformation* magazine. In addition, he has authored over 17 books on various topics of theology and is well qualified to speak on this topic. In his article, Dr. Horton calls *Jesus Calling* a 'something

more' book, an addition to the Word of God. He points out the similarities of Young's book to Andrew Murray's books and, using specific entries, assesses *Jesus Calling* as "shallow" and works oriented. The article is good and raises many questions for the reader to consider.
http://www.whitehorseinn.org/blog/2013/03/05/review-of-jesus-calling/

Toxic Devotion: A Review of Sarah Young's – Jesus Calling, by Bob DeWaay

This is one of the best and most thorough works done on *Jesus Calling* as of this date. Pastor Bob DeWaay's review was published in the summer of 2013 by Critical Issues Commentary. The author skillfully takes specific entries from *Jesus Calling* and compares them with what Scripture says. The errors are obvious and DeWaay concludes by saying that "such a book could only become a huge best-seller in an age of apostasy. It could only prosper where **sola scriptura** has been abandoned for pious feelings." This article is published in PDF form and can be acquired at the following site:
http://cicministry.org/commentary/issue125.pdf

A Christian Rebuttal to Sarah Young's Jesus Calling.

Robert Alan King makes substantive observations and expresses concerns about specific content in the devotional. He attributes *Jesus Calling* to New Age genre, but stops short of describing Sarah Young's practice as automatic writing. Mr. King describes her writings as similar to a "horoscope reading." This 16-page work is an informative expose of the many specific flaws in *Jesus Calling.* His work is published online through Amazon and also through Smashwords Edition, copyright 2011 by King and Associates. Casa Grande, AZ.

Channeling

This is an excellent resource, by Doctors John Ankerberg and John Weldon, for understanding the biblical and New Age aspects of channeling. All of the Ankerberg resources are

produced with accurate scholarship and a deep understanding of our times.
http://www.ankerberg.com/Articles/white-noise-spiritism/white-noise-spiritism%20PDF/Channeling.pdf

The Teachings of the Spirits

Again, an Ankerberg/Weldon publication. This one evaluates teachings of the spirits on the topics of Jesus, Man, Sin, Salvation, Death, and Satan. The text is well documented.
http://www.jashow.org/Articles/_PDFArchives/media-wise/MW3W0405B.pdf

Spirit Channeling

Brooks Alexander, a senior researcher for Spiritual Counterfeits Project, has written extensively on the occult. This booklet is a well-written evaluation of spiritism and the cultural ramifications of spirit channeling.

Downers Grove, IL, InterVarsity Press, 1988.

The Facts On Spirit Guides, How To Avoid The Seduction Of The Spirit World And Demonic Powers
The Facts On The New Age Movement, Answers To The 30 Most Frequently Asked Questions About The New Age Movement
The Facts On The Occult, Answers To Tough Questions About Spiritism, Occult Phenomena, And Psychic Powers
The Facts On False Teaching In The Church, What You Need To Know
The Facts On Astrology, What The Bible, Science, And Common Sense Tell Us About Astrology

These booklets, written by John Ankerberg and John Weldon and published by Harvest House Publishers, Eugene, OR, are excellent resources and supply a wealth of well-documented facts to support their allegations. These can be acquired on the Ankerberg website or Amazon.
http://www.ankerberg.com

Made in the USA
San Bernardino, CA
05 December 2013